HOMESPUN; OR, FIVE AND TWENTY YEARS AGO.

BY

THOMAS LACKLAND.

"Happy he whom neither wealth nor fashion,
Nor the march of the encroaching city,
Drives an exile
From the hearth of his ancestral homestead.

We may build more splendid habitations,
Fill our rooms with paintings and with sculptures,
But we cannot
Buy with gold the old associations."

LONGFELLOW.

"Hoc est
Vivere bis, vitâ posse priore frui."

MART. *Epigr.* XXII. 10.

NEW YORK:
PUBLISHED BY HURD AND HOUGHTON.
1867.

RIVERSIDE, CAMBRIDGE:
STEREOTYPED AND PRINTED BY
H. O. HOUGHTON AND COMPANY.

CONTENTS.

BOOK I. — Penates.

BOOK II. — Vicinage.

BOOK III. — Bucolics.

PREFACE.

IT has always fallen to the lot of Royal Families to have their historians and chroniclers, but to Farmers and plain Country People never. We have graceful descriptions of the Alhambra, as well as the history of Hampton Court, Pitti Palace, the Kremlin, and the famous Halls of the Montezumas; but few or no pens are put to service on behalf of the Farm-house, the Homestead, and the Rustic Cottage.

Much has been written and read, too, of the Boulevards and Rotten Row, of the Strand and the Corso; but little enough of quiet country roads, sequestered green lanes, cart-tracks through the woods, and winding foot-paths across the pasture-lands.

On the historic page, the Field of the Cloth of Gold makes a brilliant episode indeed; but while Homespun performs the actual service, little or nothing is said about that. The ancient Golden Fleece has been liberally talked about in mythologic history; our Golden Fleece is genuine Homespun, and that only. And we find, too, in the Greek story a great deal said in praise of the wife of Ulysses, because she pursued her spinning with such ceaseless industry; but an exceedingly small measure of panegyric is heaped on the good dames in our farm-houses of thirty years ago, because they stood at their wheels and spun the thread at home with such patience and faith.

It gives us a special delight to reflect that some of our greatest men were men of genuine homespun, — altogether domestic and simple in their character. Bred in the heart and centre of strong domestic influences, they held on by them affectionately to the last. Webster wrote home from Washington, while carrying on his broad shoulders the burdens of the State Department, for some of those beans to bake which he thought could be got nowhere out of New England. Jefferson's "Garden Book" lets us fully into the secret of his devotion to home, as his familiar letters to his daughters disclose his longings for an early return to its sincere pleasures. John Taylor of Caroline dressed in the native homespun throughout his public career, his character remaining to the last the very touchstone of simplicity and truthfulness.

The history of a household is as well worth writing as that of a kingdom, any day. Household economy is the hint and germ of the science of political economy itself. We do not see why it is not as distinctive a mark of character to be born in homespun as "in the purple"; and it is certain that more valuable men have emerged from the former than from the latter.

A dusty realm indeed must be the human heart that loves the World better than Home — politeness rather than truth — others more than its own. The man in whom the domestic feeling awaits development, is yet to discover the other hemisphere of his being. Home-life and home-love are English, — exclusive and nowise cosmopolitan; they take hold of the soil itself, and, like ivy and roses, climb to the very roof-tree. Until a man is fairly domesticated, he has not got a footing; he has not yet become his own, but is still another's; he is locked out from the enjoyment of wealth of which he is the rightful owner, unaware all the while that he carries the key in his own hand.

BOOK FIRST.

PENATES.

" *Inveni portum. Spes et fortuna, valete ; —*
Sat me lusisti, ludite nunc alios."

THRESHOLDS.

WHEN I meet a person from the country in the Bedlam of the streets, I am straightway carried back to the orchards and clover-fields, to meadows and running brooks. At once I hear calves bleat in their pens, and cattle low on the hill-side pastures. I roam in big barns, thread path-streaked timber strips, and catch the cheery sound of cock-crow in the morning.

All objects are so suggestive. My friend carries about him the scents of hay and huckleberry pastures, as well as hints of fresh butter and cheese. In him seem to be mysteriously bound up the most delightfully homelike associations, as in the thumbed leaves of some dear old book. The low and broad roof, milk-pans set against the wall in the sun, a row of hives in the sheltered corner of the little garden, apple-trees blushing with blossoms and musical with bees, doves cooing and hens cackling about the yard, winter fires of good oak and hickory on the hearth, — pictures like these all hang, in my thought, about my country friend, like the very clothes he has on, and I feel as if I must stop him short and ask him how he left the folks at home.

When the country dweller goes about building his house, the first thing he looks for, after digging his cellar, is a door-stone. Well do his far-sighted instincts tell him how smoothly the feet of gladness and grief will wear it; what light spirits are to trip across it as they enter, and what heavy burdens may be carried forth in the coming days of sorrow and separation.

The entrance to a man's house gives to the outside world much of the expression of his domestic life. He comes out on his doorstep in the moist April sunsets to listen to the chirrup of the first robin in the apple-tree, or catch the pipings of the early frogs in the marshy corner of the home lot. He gives open-handed welcomes at this point, and here he bids farewell. The eldest daughter — just married — steps over it on the blithe June morning, — and the dead child is lifted across in the sad afternoon of October. They all cluster upon it, at the return of the annual Thanksgiving; and in the Sunday mornings of summer they gather there, snapping off the spikes of lilac blossoms while they wait for the two-horse wagon to drive up and carry them to meeting.

I have, before now, unexpectedly come upon cellars of old country houses that have long ago disappeared from the landscape; the walls fallen in and mantled with weeds; no relic of a chimney standing; the smooth door-stone gone; nettles and chokeweeds growing luxuriantly in the pit; dead and drear silence brooding over the spot: — and I think that neither Marius at Carthage nor Gibbon at ruined Rome could have felt, in their way, the grief of a sadder desolation. It must be a heart unused to its own self that can confront such sights unstirred.

—— The streak of a path through the grass to the well now choked and dry; the apple-trees stinted, decayed, and blotched with cankering mosses; here and there a stone from the ruined cellar wall lying as it was thrown out; clumps of white birches and alders crowding down to the brink; no smoke curling above a bright hearth-stone; no faces eagerly pressed against window panes; no feet of children to make little prints about the door; nothing but a silence utterly voiceless all around; — a Coliseum in ruins cannot move the heart like this wreck of what was once a Home. None of the fallen arches, fragmentary columns, crumbling viaducts, or deserted London bridges could possibly suggest the outlines of a sadder story. The single cat-bird, mewing in the alders then, is more eloquent than the best inspired pens of History. Nature herself laments the end of the little drama, and with leaves and vines and greenest grasses hastens to throw over decay itself an expression of pathetic beauty.

If a Home in ruins excites feelings of such sort as this, — how easy to call back to life again the soul of a happiness now buried under the snows of many a winter's absence, which dwelt within walls that are still standing, and hallowed a spot to which the heart will remain loyal so long as it beats in the breast.

—— But thresholds are not broad, nor are people wont to tarry long upon them: — they are but for passing over. What is to be seen within, — what simple sort of life grows and ripens through the summers and winters from attic to cellar and from the front gate to the pasture bars, we will straightway go in and behold for ourselves: and on this threshold of the whole matter let me take you by the hand, gentle reader, and conduct you along.

FIRE ON THE HEARTH.

HOW little seems the gate, and how low the wall, to the one who went out but yesterday a Boy from home, and comes back again to-day a Man! There are few illusions with which the years delight to make such cruel havoc as with these of our youth.

Yet the fireplace is just as wide, and the wooden mantel as high, as when the tea-kettle used to sing on the hob in the still winter afternoons, and the old folks sat with the hickory blaze shining straight into their faces. There may have been a revolution in the house, — lifting up the ceiling, pushing back the partitions, and letting in larger windows, — but it is very pleasant to know that by the old hearth the old memories are kept sound and whole; that if they are driven down from the twilight of the garret, from the stillness of the chambers, and even out of the favorite keeping-room, they retreat as by instinct to the hearthstone, where they swarm once more in the cheery fire-blaze before flitting on clouds of smoke up the chimney, skyward.

The choicest woods to lay across the andirons are hickory and ash; they split clean and clear, the blaze they give forth is a transparent blaze, and the bed of coals they make is hard and heaping. We can sit and look into a mass of these ruddy coals for a whole evening, and feel comforted. It is Tennyson who calls for a bed of such when he says —

"Bring in great logs and let them lie,
To make a solid core of heat."

We are all of us natural fire-worshippers, — as much so as the Parsees themselves. These devotees never proffered more genuine adoration to the flames in which they saw the Soul of Light, nor did Incas below the tropics ever pay faithfuller homage to the great Sun-source of existence on solstitial mornings, than does the bleak man of bleak New England, in his inmost heart, to the honest blaze that glows and flickers over his hearth. There may be no feeling of idolatry in his love for the open fire, — but his spirit does daily and nightly offer secret sacrifice at its shrine, and in the dancing flames repeats its homebred litany.

They used to say in the old Virginia mansions that a good bright fire was the handsomest piece of furniture in the room; but, alas for it! the open door opposite was allowed to let the whole expression of comfort through. What can a house be without a fire on the hearth; and, above all, a house in the country? It is difficult to think of Home without kindling up a pleasant hearth-blaze with the thought. We search for the harmless shadows wandering up and down the walls; for the auroral flashes pulsing across the little panes in the windows, and making the home-sentiment legible. Without these, every room beneath the roof is populous with swarthy and repulsive images.

Fire is so social. It has such playful and tender sympathies, though its tongue be hot and fierce, and its maw ravenous. In the evenings, we sit down in silence before the inviting hearth, and look into its face inquiringly for revelations. We enjoy frolics with the wildest fancies, too, as they trip hither and thither across the restless waves of flame, until we give up trying to keep them company. The imagination plunges into the boiling flood of red and white heats, wallowing in its surging and retreating tides, and dragging forth drowned images, dripping from the bath of a brighter beauty. So we all love to gather around the hearth, conscious that even its dreamiest silence is intensely social.

—— But the Age we live in is an everlasting busybody. It invades every nook and corner, let it be ever so quiet and drowsy; like the tax-gatherer, it passes by no man's door. And with its many other vaunted improvements, this same Age has pushed forward an army of sappers and miners, masons and stove-fitters by name, with clinking trowels and clattering pipes, who have come and camped down in the very pleasantest rooms of all the households in the land. What with their rattling and hammering, and thumping and pounding, they have done their best to beat down and trample under foot all the tender associations that belong to the open hearth. They have drawn their curtains of sightless brick-and-mortar across the dear old fireplaces, and closed the chimney corner against spirit-visitors altogether. They have condemned all the delightful memories to a dark imprisonment, where their blackened skeletons will be found some day for the digging, overgrown with the nettleweeds and long grasses that ever make haste to beautify these homestead desolations. They have mounted a grim cylindrical invention, with the fierce, red eye of

Polyphemus, and bidden the shivering household gather around it to drive the numbness out of their fingers and the chill from their hearts: and this instrument goes by the modern name of the Stove.

—— Henceforth, Penates, away with yourselves to attic or cellar as fast as you can! You are wanted here no longer. Grandmother, in her high-crowned cap, will need to sit no more in the corner now, but must post herself in the middle of the floor rather. The smooth cedar tray, with rag-balls for the new home-made carpet, will now be kicked about under everybody's feet. There are to be no more household gatherings as of old in the evening, for the vestal fires are all gone out. A stove, you know, is not a hearth; heat is not fire; warmth is not blaze. All those brilliant crowds which came and went for us in chariots of fire, their eyes sparkling and burning from the midst of the living coals, have taken their leave forever. The cities of silver and gold that used to lie under the forestick — bristling with steeples and roofs, substantial with towers and walls, with castles and cathedrals, and washed on either side by rivers with such tides as never shone in the suns of our heaven — are faded, and darkened, and dead.

No Herculaneum was ever more oppressed with the silence which rests on its long-buried streets. The cities of the plain are not more entirely extinct and forgotten.

—— Near a blackened stove the human heart builds no altars. It sends its aspirations to heaven through no soot-begrimed pipes. It waits upon the turn of no tinman's clumsy "flues" and "dampers." Unless its sentiments be warmed in the blaze of a genial heat, they will refuse to soar on the wings of white and blue smokes skyward. Down the chimney is direct and open; but through a double-kneed stove-pipe the way is crooked and forbidding indeed. Looking up a wide-throated aperture, one may possibly catch a sky-glimpse as big as his hand; but through the narrow neck of a stove-pipe — never.

—— A Homestead without a pair of Old Folks — "Time's doting chroniclers" — seated contentedly in the chimney corner, would hardly be a homestead at all. If they are in the picture it is complete.

There you may find them, day in and day out, in all sorts of weather, steadfast to their places and to one another. When the eaves drip, in the middle of the winter forenoons, the old man with the head of silver abandons his post and the last Saturday's newspaper, to make the accustomed tour of the kitchen offices, the sheds, or the barn, lingering by the way to throw down a handful of grain for the pinched poultry. With what minuteness he is cautioned by Grandmother not to go out insufficiently clad; and with what a single-hearted joy she welcomes him when he comes back to her again! He would hardly get a warmer reception if he was just come home from a genuine polar expedition. And as soon as he has nestled down snugly in his cushioned chair once more, and dealt out on the glowing forestick a few vigorous raps with the tongs, he will launch forth into such voluble details of the keen air out doors, — suggesting Arctic reminiscences which no listener could very well call in question, — as will find the white-haired old couple topic of earnest talk till dinner is brought on the table.

The children invariably come home from school, in the wintry afternoons, to find the placid pair seated in that same accustomed spot: — the strip of sunshine lying pale and sleepily across the floor, the gray cat curled before the fire in the nest of her endless dreams, and the little sprites that are "pegged in the knotty entrails" of the oak logs singing the drowsy hours away. Wilkie would have made the picture immortal. Down along the snowy roads the winds are wrestling with travellers, pulling and tearing at hats, and cloaks, and meagre robes; — but no winds are to be felt in this room's tranquil haven; here all days are halcyon days, and no atmosphere is breathed but that of peace and heaven. In the old man's cheeks the rich mottle is as fresh, to appearance, as it ever was; the features betray no look of being pinched with the cold; no snows can get in to benumb his attenuated fingers.

They two constitute a sort of family tribunal; and a highly useful arrangement it is, in a crowded domestic congress. They are always to be found on the judicial bench, ready to give audience. Many are the tough little problems that are brought to them for their wise solution. They pass upon cases in which the interests of the turbulent younglings are involved, with a promptness which challenges the disputants' wonder; and if Grandma only *said* thus and so, there is no use in hunting for higher authority, — she is conceded to be the "end of the law." Or Grandpa promises to mend the broken sled; and never was sled of boy repaired with greater dexterousness and ingenuity. From early morning until nightfall he rambles about the house on short excursions, filled full and thoroughly warmed with the dear home feeling.

—— And when one pair of dimmed eyes becomes yet dimmer, and at last fades entirely from the hearth, — and one stooping form is carried forth from its cherished corner to be seen there no more forever, — what vacancy in the heart of the household then! Looking up from her forenoon occupation, Grandmother throws her eyes, from sheer force of habit, into the opposite corner; but the chair stands empty over there, and a great tear trembles on her cheek as she adjusts her needle in the knitting-sheath she wears. The fire is not so hot that it can warm her chilled heart any longer. She listens to the wintry winds that are blowing without, — and thinks of that single grave, freshly rounded under the pines.

—— It is at night that the hearth shows in its true glory. The fire-spirits seem to love best to assemble then. In those late days of Autumn, when the evenings are grown perceptibly longer, and the cricket sings in the corner as if he were hoarse, and the sodden leaves lie thickly trampled in the walks and yard, — the first blaze of a fire on the hearth is very welcome, for it is a summons to all the accustomed worshippers to gather again at the family shrine; and it distinctly holds out pleasant promises that cluster, like ripe ivy berries, about the long months of the winter. There is just enough chill in the air to drive one to the fire; and on the hearth is just enough fire to make the chill enjoyable. Through the round of the whole year, I know no other fires like this first hearth-blaze in the Autumn. The group of Winter delights shines out then, as upon a canvas.

The chief treasure of our winters is buried in the depth of the long evenings. Father and Mother are early in their places, and the children range themselves conveniently around. No matter what the peculiar employments of the time, the associations that clothe all are of a really sacred character. The masks which each may have worn through the day, unlace then and fall off. Face answers to face, as heart silently speaks to heart. The round world has no enticements to offer, so simple and true as those of the wintry fire-light. Men afterwards throw back longing glances from the advanced paths of their feverish life-career to an innocent picture like this, and in their hearts confess it is the very realization of which they are striving to be possessed. Yet they drift further and further from it instead, till nothing remains of the picture but the picture, its outlines fading into faintness, and with little life in its body save what a jaded memory has it in its power to supply.

The smoky stories that go with these evening delights at the hearth are not to be set down as the days are in the calendar: — they are gypsy children of the peaceful hours themselves, and troop forth only at such times as they are wanted. The ancient Dutch tiles are not half so crowded with their Scripture illustrations as are our commonest old fireplaces with scenes that illustrate these homely winter-evening stories. The youngest boy of all is not more under the spell than his eldest brother. They climb the stairs to bed, at last, in strange enough company. The girls feed the coals with wisps of paper, and watch, while the sparkles travel up and down the burnt heap, to "see the folks go home from meeting." A genuine ghost story instantly makes the logs populous; the shadowy faces of spirits peer from mysterious caverns among the sticks; their impalpable forms flit across weltering seas of flame, climb nimbly into towers and steeples, and beckon at windows through which pour the floods of yellow sunsets.

All this, and many, many times more, can a story of some sleepless ghost evoke from the logs that were so lately chopped on the old wood lot.

—— At the hearth, the heart seems to bind up all its sheaves for harvest. There all its joys — domestic and foreign — are gathered in. There the sombre woof is gaily shot with bright figures and patterns. The self-communion at this altar is searching and thorough. A man sits down face to face with himself, and would love to think no more of the world or its guile.

If there might be a hearth in every heart! And the precious memories which one brings away with him, too, seasoned well with time, rich with ripened colors, and mellow with flavors that cannot be described!

The fireplace has been the district schoolhouse for the discipline of the present generation in the virtues they possess, whether few or many. What is tender in popular sentiment — what is simple and direct in popular preaching and speaking — what is strong and homely and well-grounded in popular phrase, has its healthy and enduring root here. Tear up all the broad hearth-stones in the land to-day, and these very memories would start at once, like tender grasses, around them, to beautify the spot whence they sprung and keep them green forever.

RAINY DAYS.

WHEN I go off into the country to stay awhile, I like, of all things, on pulling the bedclothes about me and settling my head in the pillows for the night, to hear the rain drip from the eaves on the roof of the porch. The sound makes the sense of comfort and cosiness full and complete. If I were sure the world was to be drowned out before morning, it would scarcely ruffle the serenity of my spirit one whit. I lie and let flow through my mind unformed fancies of tall, feathery brakes, pearly with rows of rain-drops, emptying their leafy buckets into my boot-tops; of drenched boughs in the woods, slapping their showers in my neck and face; of mill-dams carried off by rising floods; of bridges gone, and deluges working down between the singing shingles into the room: — but the effort, somehow, is after a time too great, and I sink to slumber among the murmurs of the rain as tranquilly as a child goes off, with its last plaything held tight in its little hand.

They have no real rainy days in the city. What are so styled are only dark days — dirty days — days of mud, and slosh, and soured tempers — days of soggy boots, saturated clothes, and spoiled hats. In the country, Nature makes nothing of showing you her face; and it is not lowery and scowling, either, — it is tearful, more or less "blubbered," as Spencer would say, yet altogether placid and calm underneath. The rain is no more than a changing mood there, which she comes out of all the happier for having submitted to its brief obscuration.

It is not an easy matter to say if any two individuals, harbored by chance in the same shelter, get just the same sort of experience out of a rainy day. I have been a patient listener to many a personal narrative on this theme, but every one, I found, was the property of its owner alone. The heavens, therefore, do not rain down the same influences upon us all.

Then, too, rain affects us differently in different places. It is one thing if you are sheltered snugly and warm at home, at the opening of a gray November storm, such as hoods the New England hills with its weird-looking mists, — and quite another if you happen to be weather-bound in some far back little country tavern, with a dismally long day ahead, and only a checker-board, a foul stove, and a handful of water-soaked idlers for social consolation. One could make himself very happy at home, with dog and cat and books and family close about him; but in these by-places, the sentiment seems to get rubbed off by the dirty clothes, and trampled to death under the muddy boots.

But ah! it is so delicious to the spirit that is at all sensitive, to hear the big drops pattering on the roof; the garret is the place to get true inspiration from the rain. What hidden realms of pleasure the boys and girls explore up there, rummaging the old place from end to end! Side-saddles and antique bonnets are dragged forth from their twilight domains, to do service once more for a generation undreamt of in the day of their original glory. Faded out pamphlets, and books with half covers, — perhaps a fragment of old Flavius Josephus, or the remnant of an odd volume of Colonial History, or, more likely, a pile of preserved almanacs, inlaid and overlaid with dust and diligently eaten of rats, — fan the embers of the childish thought into a living flame, and the afternoon hours glide away as silently as the twilight owl sails off into the mystery of a deeper darkness. The Saturday afternoons in old garrets are well-nigh sacred, for the memories that are stored within them; and the mere mention of them along with the rain is enough to bring back a lost man entirely to himself again.

Rainy days at home are apt, likewise, to put in the head a vagabondish wish for a thoughtful ramble over the domestic premises. It is a fatuity with me then to go poking into every odd and curious corner there is; in my mind, an indefinable association links out-of-the-way house-nooks and rainy days together. To stand idly at the back door and listen to the water rilling into the hogshead at the corner, is a good deal better than Casta Diva; and the melodies stick faster in the heart. Around the back buildings and under the sheds huddle the poultry, with drooping tails and drowned feet, watching the sprinkle of the rain and listening to its sounds, till they fall asleep on foot, at last, from the sheer narcotism of its monotony. The house dog walks from the barn to the shed, and from the shed to the kitchen, occasionally throwing up a weatherwise eye at the clouds, as if he were wondering when it would clear off again. The cows are gone under the barn for a while, and there they quietly ruminate and grow steamy. The horse looks cautiously out of his stall window, becomes disheartened with the prospect, and draws his long face in again.

—— As soon as the Spring buds are ready to burst in millions of little green parachutes, and the brooks are rising and rinsing out the gullies, and the trout leap eagerly for the stray tributes of fortune that come swimming down, — none of the common pleasures known are matched by that of being out in the rain. The drizzle is truly delightful. Aquarius himself ought then to confess himself satisfied. The fine rain seems to work its way into the very pores, and refreshes as well as equalizes the animal spirits.

With this weather the noise of running brooks is in perfect tune. In the low, alluvial tracts sprout sheaves of rank marsh plants of gigantic promise, among such weeds as people these swampy regions. The drops of rain fringe the black birch and alder boughs like lines of bells, dripping from them in rows with the slightest shaking. The torpid old fisherman, like the sun-loving turtle, may be seen glued to the rock by the pond-side, waiting patiently for bites and a precarious dinner; yet if you go and sit down beside him in his own spirit, he will let you further into the still secrets of Nature — concerning fish, new moons, mink traps, high waters, woodcraft, and river lore — than you could extract from all the poets in a three months' reading; and it will be wholly fresh and reliable, with the earthy smell to it, too.

A gray and sullen November rain, coming down over the hills as if it meant to seize and wrap you in its chilly folds, has its really charming side, too. It is good to be out on the hill-side pastures then. The brown and matted grasses, the faded ferns, the stripped trees, the straggling sheep huddled under the lee of the stone wall, and the woodland dimly receding like a ship at sea in the dense fog, start around the thought a crowd of familiar associations. Home comforts take shape instantly in the mind, and the winter landscape before the imaginary view grows green in the prospect of its recurring pleasures. There is a mysterious power in these autumn rains to shut one up within himself, which begets the cosy feeling that attends upon their approach; and if we come nearer still and look close enough, we can detect, if we cannot trace, the secret law that holds our souls to the heart of Nature.

The falling rains of this season find stout

piles of wood about the sheds, ready for the ringing axe of December, when the mercury is low and the blood needs a start in the veins. They drive vainly against the many-paned homestead windows, and now and then force themselves in a little, before they are over. They drip, and keep dripping, from the boughs of the big elm before the house, and give a sorry look to the apple trees behind it.

And then the barns, too, swarm with associations that are filled with a wonderful magnetism. The broad bay is heaped full, and the staunch scaffolds overhang with their sweet-scented burthen. The poultry go slying about the dry floors, and in and out the secret nooks made by the hay, pecking at stray seeds and very happy in their security from the storm without. The cows are contented to stay late in their stalls in the morning, nor will they go far from the door even when let out. Occasionally, an old cat, with a half-wild expression, crosses the mow up under the ridge-pole, making rustling footfalls that break the silence ominously.

On rainy days, the old home-kitchens, so spacious and clean, are alive with domestic enterprises of every device and description; and if it so chances that it is the baking-day, the scene can hardly be matched anywhere for its industry. Bowls and trays and long wooden spoons — iron kettles stuffed with rye-and-indian dough — pies by the dozen, and joints all ready and waiting for the spit; fire on the hearth, and fire wandering to and fro over the concave of the great brick oven; mingled scents of all good things baking and simmering; every one busy and intensely interested; and the whole presenting a picture of a domestic laboratory, in which choicest gratifications are secured for every variety of appetite. None save the well-ordered and thorough country household can present an exhibit of this sort; and then it becomes one of the most substantial of home attractions.

It is an indescribable pleasure, likewise, to be out riding in the rain, if the long country roads are any way passable; shut in from the reach of storm and wind, snug and dry as a mouse in a Cheshire cheese, your horse sure-footed and his face set homewards, — you feel a glow of satisfaction even in the spongiest of days, and while driving between dark stone walls and drowned reaches of woodland. It gives me a secret pleasure then to roll past lordly farm-houses, catching glimpses of smoking cattle about the barn doors, or signs of inquisitive human life at the front windows; or sounds of responsive threshing-flails from the barns on far-off hill-sides, of barking watch-dogs, and shrill chanticleer in the pauses. All the more welcome and cheery is it then, because Home is ahead, with its bright fires, and loving faces, and dry comforts uncounted.

—— There is no reason why a storm of rain should be a spell of gloom, to be grumbled through as we get through the annual Fast Day of the Governor. Why do we choose to be no better than barometers, — such sensitive children of the weather? Why should we consent to let the clouds make or mar our happiness? Does not the sun shine at the centre of our being forever? It ought rather to be that rainy days, by the mysterious aid of their associations, bring us into closer and better acquaintance with ourselves, external attractions having for the time parted with the most of their power; and, in this better sense, are they to be offered a hail and a welcome, and even hoarded with those golden strips and margins of our existence, when we journey more parasangs than on any other. At home, they serve to wash the heart clean of its worldliness, even as they wash the windows with their welcome flood.

GARDEN WORK.

"GOD Almighty first planted a Garden," says Bacon, "and, indeed, it is the purest of human pleasures; it is the greatest refreshment to the spirits of man."

"There is no ancient gentlemen," says the grave-digger in Hamlet, "but gardeners, ditchers, and grave-makers; they hold up Adam's profession."

Said the gentle old Archbishop Sancroft to his friend Hough, who was visiting him in Suffolk: "Almost all you see is the work of my own hands, though I am bordering on eighty years of age. My old woman does the weeding, and John mows the turf and digs for me; but all the nicer work — the sowing, grafting, budding, transplanting, and the like — I trust to no other hand but my own, so long, at least, as my health will allow me to enjoy so pleasing an occupation."

—— The Poets are full of the delights of gardening; Cowley and Pope, at least, came to realize their dreams in this respect. One can run through very few pages of English verse, and not have to leap hedges of allusions to gardens, or without bringing away a memory stuck full with their fragrant blossoms. An appreciative writer observes that "Bacon and Milton were the prophet and the herald, Pope and Addison the reformer and the legislator, of horticulture." Spenser's stanzas abound with real garden pictures, terrace raised above terrace, and lawn stretching beyond lawn. The garden scene in "Romeo and Juliet" is the favorite one with all readers, because in the fragrant atmosphere of the garden, in the tempered moonlight, and to the sound of trickling waters, love is made in the true spirit of romance. Tennyson has shown us how it is attempted in the more exquisite passages of his everywhere-quoted "Maud." The poet Shenstone wrote from his favorite Leasowes: "I feed my wild ducks, I water my carnations; happy enough if I could extinguish my ambition quite." Father Adam was placed in a garden to "dress and keep it." Every reader of English recalls at once Milton's fine description of our first parents in Eden, rising with the dawn, to dress the alleys green, —

"Their walk at noon, with branches overgrown."

The gray old monks, in fact, who had an eye open to the good things of life in their day, were the first genuine cultivators of flowers and fruits, and around their solitary keeps of learning slept securely many a productive garden and blossoming orchard. They had the true relish for what those things brought them, and tended a tree or a flower with the same zeal with which they wore the pavement smooth with their frequent devotions. They taught us horticulture, and we are thus become their debtors for more than the mere learning they were instrumental in handing down.

—— The sincerest pleasures of the home-life are woven closely in with those of the garden. I have almost made one of my own heart, from the habit of living over again the delight I used to take in digging, planting, weeding, and watering the little half-acre Elysium, where grew so luxuriantly my bulbous cabbages and bright-eyed beans. I am conscious that Goëthe did not miss of the general truth in his observation that he took the solidest delight in the simplest pleasures; and, for an enduring pleasure, clean and sweet both in itself and its memories, we can truly think of nothing in Nature before a little garden. It should not be so large as to become a task-master, and thus worry out the placid zeal; but only spacious enough to excite the physical energy and give a healthy start to the thought.

I am not making any allusion to city gardens now, nor to their more luxuriantly gay cousins of the suburbs, where the owner is far from being the author, but employs his gardener as many a man does his upholsterer; those make beautiful "estates," and are objects of attraction alike to shrewd brokers and fashionable lovers of Nature; but they have few of the savory associations of simplicity, and peace, and home. Fine enough exotics may grow and show there, whose health and beauty salaried gardeners look carefully after; but you will search in vain for simple morning-glories, climbing like eager children to the window-sill to peep in, or for snowy caps out among the bean-poles in the delicious summer weather.

Work, before breakfast, in the retired garden-spot is a sort of inspiration for the rest of the day. In that still hour, you mark how your lettuce and cabbages have shot up during the night, and at once renew your faith in Nature. I fear my closest friend would have failed to recognize me then, as I used to look in that patched and shredded apparel, the limp hat-rim falling down about my face and eyes, and on my knees, too, — before many others were, — for striped bugs and green cabbage-worms.

Or, next to the early morning work, with the dewy earth offering its grateful exhalations to the nostrils, the twilight stroll through the limited grounds is full of peaceful delight, and tends to provoke contemplation. If you were in the morning the *laborer*, you can realize that you are the lord at evening; going about and pulling up scattered weeds, perhaps changing around a few plants, thinning the sprouted rows of beets or onions, grubbing up some pestiferous root, or planning somewhat for the next morning's industry.

In all the old-fashion gardens one finds a double row of currant bushes, almost as inevitable as the lilac or the white rose-bush, at the garden gate. A charming alley is thus opened up for nearly the length of the plat. They maintain their lines as faithfully as appointed metes and bounds; and, spread over the green ruffles of their leaves, may be seen, all through the season, a white crop of old ladies' caps, that tells of the grandmother whose hand planted the purple morning-glories under the windows, and whose head now and then shows itself between the verdurous walls of the bean-vines. A man would as soon think of tearing a true sentiment out of his heart, if such a thing could be done, as of pulling up the currant bushes that are so well rooted in the garden.

How the red beet-tops glisten in their long rows, as if some pains-taking hand had varnished them, one by one! How crowded stand those carrots, boring each its long yellow fingers into the mellowed subsoil! With what a Dutch-like and dogmatic air the swelling cabbages erect their pulpy heads in the performance of the useful work they are set to do!

At the further end of the plat stands the summer-house, — a sort of Pomona's shrine, in its way, as well as a moonlight resort for lovers; a contorted grape-vine weaving a lattice of leaves below and a canopy of green overhead, whose purple tributes you may sit and pluck in the dreamy afternoons of September, while the yellow finches are clustering on the bushes and the poultry are wallowing in the soft garden mould.

—— Daybreak, in summer, is a fresh experience every morning, in the garden. A good deal has been said, good and bad, about the glories of that hour on the hill-top and at the riverside; but in the seclusion of the leafy little patch beside the homestead it is, apparently, not so well known. If one only *has* a garden in which to offer salutation to the day-god, he has at least one more inducement to get out of bed in the dewy hours of the morning. To be right in the midst of your own growing vegetables; to behold the favorite sunflowers all turned to the east; to watch the bean-sprouts, coming up with their twin leaves out of the cleft heart of the seed; to shave down ranks of red-stemmed weeds with a single sweep of the bright hoe; to brush your peas, pole your beans, set frames to support your cucumbers and tomatoes, trim your young hedges, hunt the bugs among the squash vines, and plan new paths through beds of vegetables and rows of fruit-trees: — this it is to seize a fresh pleasure in the very bloom of its freshness, and load the heart with a harvest of memories that grow all the more fragrant with age.

Somehow, the poets have linked all the pleasant names with the pleasant occupations. Therein they have shown themselves *to be* poets. The very word Garden is laden, like a wain, with bundles of blossoming associations. When men speak of subduing the rugged wildness of Nature, the phrase goes that they will make it "beautiful as a *garden*." In gardens live buds and blossoms, along with the bees and the sunshine; and they die there, too. They lie close to Home. We step from the kitchen door through the garden gate. Peaches ripen on their walls; and blooming plums drop plump on their mellow soil. Our feet loiter in their delightful walks, and the atmosphere breathes only contentment and peace.

In gardening, and its cognate associations, we get away from the hot fuming of the world and go back to the cool and shaded bowers of simplicity and truth. We seem to stand with uncovered heads in the porch of Nature's great temple. We smell savors as fresh as the morning dews and as sweet as the breath of the rustling corn. There is such a retired, such a cool, such a far-off look from the outer world to the heart of the garden, that one deplores the necessity that takes him away from so peaceful a pursuit, and wonders if there may not come a time when he shall stay at home altogether in his rustic corner, and dress and keep his little garden-spot to the end of his days.

—— When the pale autumn suns fall aslant

through the dried stalks, and little flocks of birds flutter here and there over the grounds in quest of seeds that have burst their pods, and tomatoes lie red and glossy among the wilted and fallen vines, and bean-pods hang from the poles without green leaves to shelter them any longer, and slender-waisted wasps find their way to the decayed fruits that lie, here and there, over the ground, — the thoughts are allured by every object to the tenderest mood of contemplation; the very atmosphere is full of the realization of pleasant dreams. These particular days in the garden have charms which are not matched even by the glimpses of glory furnished in the spring.

He who loves the home-spot then finds employments after his heart's desire. To gather and garner — to pull the rich roots out of the ground where they have waxed fat through a whole season's dirty idleness — to get in the beans, the peppers, the mangoes, and such other vegetables as ripen in seed-vessels — to go from garden to barn, from barn to kitchen, from kitchen to cellar, and so back to the garden again, keeps the feelings of the domesticated man in a state of contented pleasure all the while, and renews the ties continually that hold him to the home he loves.

The poultry run in and out before him, and the season's chickens delight to wallow in the loosened dirt under the lee of the fence, stretching their yellow legs in the genial sun. Grandmother's bed of marigolds awaits the clipping of her shears, and looks like a shoal of bright fish, dyed in the yellow stream of some Pactolus. As for the rows of sturdy-looking winter cabbages, they may stand out awhile through the fall frosts, and even get powdered with the first light snows of November; — and the growing turkey-poults may peck at the loose outside leaves on their way to roost in the apple-trees.

One cannot think of the Spring house-cleaning, without a revived reminiscence of the early garden-work, too. The boys are raking the rubbish from the grass and the beds, and setting fire to it in the piles they have heaped up around; into which the old shoes of the past year are thrown as burnt-offerings. The girls are at the posies, scratching away like so many hens in the high tide of mischief. The dog has his nose in every nook, new or old, that is to be found. The windows are all opened, to let in the genial sun. Bees drive across the yards, impatiently foraging for the first blossoms. The robins make the air vocal with their welcome calls, and are scouting about the plantations for nice places to build their nests. The sprouted sprays of the old elm on the lawn are pencilled on the ground in the sunshine, with the utmost minuteness. All about the premises there are the joyous sights and sounds of Spring, bringing glad tidings of the new life that has suddenly broken over the world.

—— And this is the life of Home. Has the whole world any thing to offer that is debased with so little alloy ?

But finest of all, and crown of all the home glories, are the roses ; those beautiful children of the dews and sun ; clambering in such wild riotousness about the porch, and thrusting their boquets of red-and-white in at the windows ; cloudy masses of colors just fetched from Paradise, mingled as if in chance drifts, and piled against the house like snows against the walls in winter ! The little parlor — shaded and low — is filled with the breath of their very hearts. Through the whole of June, the dear old place is a sort of Dreamland. In the most brilliant colorings of oriental tales — in the dreamiest pictures of islands in the southern seas, nothing so satisfies the imagination and the heart as the luxuriant rose-vines, bossed from root to crown with glories of buds and blossoms; lavishing their sweet lives on the happiness of those who dwell contentedly at home; and conjuring up for soul and sense, through the magic of color and perfume, ideal scenes that line the roadways of life with banks of ravishing fragrance and bowers of beauty without end.

—— The Rose is the Angel of the Garden; and one can therefore readily comprehend what the poet Gray meant when he exclaimed —"Happy they who can create a Rose!" Sir Henry Wotton wrote of it, in his verses "On his Mistress, the Queen of Bohemia," —

"You Violets that first appear,
By your pure purple mantles known,
Like the proud virgins of the year,
As if the Spring were all your own, —
What are you when the ROSE is blown?"

SUNDAY IN THE COUNTRY.

OF the almost silent delights of this one day out of the seven, those who persistently dwell in the cities know little or nothing. The few whom the heat or the fashion drives forth into still country neighborhoods for two or three weeks each summer, carry back with them but a half-notion of the Country Sunday as it is, — albeit they are as fond of talking about it as if they were as steady to meeting as the deacons themselves. It is a clear mistake to suppose that one little foray into the country, every summer, is going to supply a requisite idea of ordinary country matters: — a man may as well make his choice of a house by sample.

That sort of country life which neighbors upon the cities, whose sober warp is shot daily with the gay woof of town travel, is not the life I am speaking of now; in the quiet rural retirement where I write, I hear no roar of car wheels or shrill whoop of the steam-whistle even in the distance. I fail to see glittering turn-outs on their way to church, to upset the sober heads of such as gather on the village Green. The charm of it is, the country at no time loses its real country character. The Sunday morning air is as tranquil, and in summer as redolent, as the poets all say it was in Eden. You can hear mellow bells calling one to another from hill-top to hill-top, their echoes tripping across the intervening meadows as lightly as tricksy Ariel. Men, women and children are starched up in their very cleanest and best. An open wagon, stiffly set on the old-fashion "thorough-braces," comes as near to a coupé, chariotee, or barouche as you can ordinarily discover. Everybody is plain, homely, and remarkably sober. Everybody travels the lengthening roads to meeting because, primarily, it is a duty, and not merely a sentiment, or the fashion. Underneath a fixed rigidity their hard, dry humor is effectually covered up; and only at the noon intermission of an hour, — behind the meeting-house, perhaps, or just around the next corner, or tucked away in the half-shadows of the horse-sheds, — do the men dare to relax their muscles from the set Sunday grimness, and give way to an outbreak of humor at best almost as sickly as the sun seen through a bit of smoked glass.

There are, to be sure, some interior villages all along the lines of the railroads, that hold up their heads on a Sunday with a good deal of pert pretension; but these cannot deny, if they would, that they are still fastened by the umbilical cord to the city systems and customs. Such are not — mind you — your genuine *country* villages, that have from the start set up housekeeping for themselves, "do" their own washing and ironing, and cut and make their own clothes. If one desires to see and enjoy the real country Sunday, he must go off beyond city reach altogether.

In New England, these choice places that I am talking of may still be found in plenty, cut up as the surface of the country is with railroads; but you cannot expect to see them by merely looking out of a flying car window. They are to be sought, and not stumbled upon. If you once start out on foot, almost any crooked by-road will beguile you towards them with certainty.

In the summer time, when the sun gets up and looks in at the east windows, not far from half-past four o'clock of a Sunday morning, the good farmer-folk bestir themselves right early. In place of setting the pitcher in the dingy area for the milk-and-water man, they turn out to fill their own frothy pails as soon, certainly, as sunrise, and send off the dewy-coated cows to pasture again. The children are all brought up to the kitchen sink, and scrubbed and rubbed till they take on a shine like new furniture. Pretty soon old aunts slip out into the garden and snap off a spike or two of lilac blossoms from the bush close by the gate, which they stick into broken-nosed pitchers about the mantels and hearth. The farmers themselves, in snowy shirt-sleeves, are everywhere about the barns, greasing up the wagon wheels, tinkering at the harnesses, and indulging in a general fuss of preparation for the hour of meeting.

Not a home in the whole breadth of quiet landscape but is at that moment all ready to send forth its own swarm. And the white wooden meeting-house is big enough to collect and hold them all safely together.

Breakfast being done, and the children having taken off their long tires, a tedious spell — to them — intervenes till church time. Where the family is a pious and well-ordered one, the restless young folks are seated around the room in a silent circle, generally with Testaments in their hands; and there they keep them fast, sitting stiffly, primly, and uncomfortably, until *the* hour comes laggingly around. No matter if a golden-ringed humblebee does fly in at the open window; or a lady butterfly shakes the yellow dust from the velvet of her gorgeous cloak, just over the window-sill; or a bird comes and sings on a low bough hard by, to let the boys feel how unspeakably joyous outdoor liberty must be, of a Sunday morning: — there must they sit all in a row, with faces as rigid as the copies of Miles Standish's, and spirits crowded back into the pit of youthful despair, till the old clock in the corner rings out ten, and perhaps a little while after.

After the country wagons begin to stir the dust on the roads, they do not stop to let it settle again. One family party close behind another; a white horse pulling up behind a red one, and a lean beast chasing after a pot-bellied one; a loitering line of sturdy young fellows, honest and lusty, whose necks and hands have been tanning all the week in the hot corn-fields; now two maidenly women in bonnets to match their years, — now a hobbling old man who is not able to keep a horse, turning about all the while to let the wagons pass him; girls crowded in on the back seats at the cost of much of the starch in their Sunday attire; — these are the sights that give a new face, on that day, to the landscape. You see nothing like it near the cities; you would hardly think that such pictures could be sketched from life anywhere.

Almost every country meeting-house has a plat of green grass before and around it; and, occasionally, a few trees, — old elms, or vigorous growing maples. Commonly, too, a sign-post,—the magnet for knots of men before services open within, whereon they attentively study the probate, town, and society's proclamations.

It is painfully clear that nobody feels at his ease in his Sunday clothes; the efforts to appear so only make the fact more apparent. This one is in a sorry state of doubt about the best place for his hands, and you guess he wishes he could have left them at home. That one puts little faith in his feet, thrusting forth first one and then the other, as if they were in conspiracy to play him false and let him down. A third betrays his slight personal acquaintance with the hat he wears that day, continually tipping it back and pulling it forward upon his head. Still another goes around offering his hand to everybody, as if he thought there must be some magic in the town's palms. The uneasiest and unhappiest one of all laughs when he catches anybody else laughing, though he can give no sort of reason why he should.

If one of the other sex chances to pass him on her way in, he begins with throwing a glance at her sneakishly, and ends with a square and courageous turn-about, studying the motions of her shoes till they take her up the steps and out of his sight.

And they will show just as sober over these matters as if none could be more serious among the concerns of the world. But then, their humor is sober, and hard, and bald, even on week-days; they do not give it stretch and play by social contact; and hence their Sunday spirits are dashed with a kind of gloom it would be a hard matter to describe. Why this is really so, — why Sunday and a dejected countenance should so regularly come together in rustic experience, I am sure mine is not the gift to divine. One would think it ought to be just otherwise. To know a visible God in the new blessing of the morning sunshine, in the dense and cool shadows of the trees, in the meadows, spread with their carpets of living green, and in the broad fields of corn with their ten thousand lances tilting in the early breeze; to catch His benignant smile breaking out over the hill-sides, over the crests of the rolling tree-tops, and in the far-off blue of the heavens; to hear His voice in every one of the sounds of air and earth, and to feel profoundly the influence of His presence, like that of the very atmosphere, all around you, — *this* is what Sunday might be to every man that lives, and what it surely ought to be; and this it will be, too, when we awake to the visions which a truly spiritual life scatters so plentifully around us.

—— As *I* look at such matters, nothing sweeter, or purer, or more delicious to a simple soul, can be conceived than the unaffected singing of a Country Choir. There is so little scientific fuss and professional palaver about it. And the melodies come out so full and clear, — a creation each by itself, rising and falling in its cadences like the steady swell of the sea! I know few things, for myself, more true and hearty. There stands the choral row, male and female, heads erect and mouths opened wide, letting out souls and voices together; the fiddle squeaking with excitement to get the lead, and the hard-working chorister, with quick eye thrown to one side and the other, actually singing down the whole! As for the melody itself, — so simple and direct, so plaintive, so stirring, filling the house as with a flood from floor to ceiling, and drifting out through the opened doors and windows into the echoing street, — it is enough to move the most worldly heart that ever tried to mint itself into money. One hardly thinks he catches such seraphic strains again, though he goes all the way from New England to Rome.

Then, too, a genuine country parson's sermon is nothing like a city clergyman's discourse; and if you go into the interior to hear one, you must not expect to find it so. Not generally is much attention paid to verbal tactics, or to rhetorical ornaments, or to brilliancy of metaphor. The people who listen want about so much plain talk, and so much old-fashion, hammer-and-tongs logic; as for the rest, it is all "leather and prunella." In truth, I grieve to tell that a good many of the pulpits, in this last respect, have grown to be hardly better than scolding-blocks. Some of the men-hearers sit in their shirt-sleeves, in downright hot weather, and some are drowsing and nodding as if in Elysium already. The sixthlies, lastlies, and finallies come along after the former fashion, and find them, as the Master found the disciples of old time, fast asleep. Even the preacher, banging the dust with such zeal out of the faded cushion, is not able to shatter or scatter their soothing Sabbath dreams. Poor brethren! they are guilty of no sort of fault; so very hard has been their work in the week's open air, when they come to sit down in close meeting on Sunday, it is the easiest matter in the world to fall asleep! So sweet must that sleep always be; — how dare any self-righteous looker-on, with his mind off the sermon, say it is an ungodly one!

The children lay their heads in their mothers' laps, and shortly forget who they are or why they came. The women — some of them — nibble somewhat slyly at bunches of fennel and dill, glance down on their slumbering offspring, and fall to a fresh survey of one another. In the galleries, the larger boys spread themselves over the seats and benches, and beguile the heavy hour with studying the faces of the congregation below, or watching for the last leaf of the lengthening sermon. Out-of-doors, the horses stamp resentfully under the sting of summer flies, and, now and then, a motherly old mare sends forth a shrill whinny for the young colt that followed her from manger to meeting. If, now, a stranger, entirely unused to such scenes, could be taken up bodily out of the noisy world and dropped into a spot like this, it would impress him with such a sentiment as Sabbath never left upon his heart before. He would almost be driven to wonder where he had been, and what he had been doing, all his days, that he had never yet learned to "keep" Sunday as it ought to be kept indeed.

—— A long time after service, you may see persons strolling up and down the street, talking in low and subdued voices. The air holds, as Gray says, a "solemn stillness." The vane on the meeting-house steeple seems to swim in the sky. Swallows are cleaving the air in chase of evening insects, and emitting that quick "chip-chip" of a cry which is all they have to offer for an evening song. Boys — barefoot now, but otherwise in their "Sunday best" still — come driving home a cow or two apiece from the near pastures. About their back doors women are making ready for their next day's washing, setting tubs and pails where they will be handiest in the early morning. So silent are the untravelled country roads now, streaked with tracks of green grass as they are, and ruled in with stone walls all spattered with mosses, — the soothing delight of loitering over them at this contemplative hour can be described by a comparison with no other known to the worshipful heart.

—— But this is the summer picture. In winter, matters take on a sensible change.

In the first place, it is noticeable enough that it makes all the difference whether the earth wears a garment of grass or a white robe of snow. Next, it is sleighs, instead of wagons, that bring the good farmers' families over to meeting, whose styles are as varied as the dates on which ambitious workmen gave them a launch into travelling existence. Green sleighs and yellow ones, — high backs and low, — cutters and pungs, — they slip along over the smooth road with a living freight full as miscellaneous as the conveyances themselves are oddly assorted. The girls and boys are passionately fond of this mode of travel, whether it is Sunday or not. Brighter than the shining of the snow upon the ground is the sparkle of their eyes. The jingle of the straps of deep-toned bells around the horses' necks and bellies, wakes them as thoroughly as the fife and drum at May training.

It is a point of horsemanship with every young fellow who brings a girl along to meeting with him, to "cut a dash" or execute some sort of "curly Q" with his steed, as he drives him up before the door; and the serious antics of some of the venerable old plough-horses, coming up to the steps with curbed neck and tossing tails, are enough to crimson even a jaundiced face with laughter. There in the sleigh-box, how snug and cosily they are squeezed together under the shaggy robes! What an expression — half apology and half bluster — the gallant young reinsman wears on his face, as he proceeds to hand out his lady with such a substantial *jump* upon the steps! Behold! — alas, poor human nature! — the less fortunate wights who stand around, *nudging* one another in a sort of jealous derision, and making almost superhuman efforts to feel that *they* would not be concerned in that kind of business for half the entire town, — girls and all!

Through the forenoon services, no greater discomfort can be imagined than to have to sit in a corner furthest from the stove; but by afternoon, the blue chill wears away a little. Still, a fan in one's hand would be not much more than a vain ornament even then. Many straggle off to huddle close about the hot stove, where they complete the work of baking their heads, acquire red and heavy eyes, and discover that the discourse from the pulpit is a world too deep for them. The rising winter wind blows from every side against the old structure, straining its venerable joints and racking its whole frame in resistance; now it goes whistling through the crevices of the multiplied windows in a merry tune, and now it falls to scolding and howling like a fury to protest that it will not be shut out.

In the evening — for country folk keep Saturday rather than Sunday night — the beaux are about, furnished with horses and sleighs, bells and all. They do their courting on Sunday evenings only, and on alternate weeks at that; but they make their hours so late that they could well afford to crowd the two evenings into one. With all their natural flow of spirits, a more serious class of acquaintances, when out on these agreeable excursions, no rustic young lady could lay claim to; brave enough, they may be, on ordinary occasions, but at these particular times the very bashfullest of cowards. And the girls sit and wait so impatiently for the ring of the bells, — for do you suppose they cannot distinguish even the sound of the bells about the necks of their lover's horses? They have made up a bright fire in the "keeping-room" on purpose, and are bringing their feelings into a state of as high effervescence as the acquaintance will allow. Do you ask if they feel the *cold* in that rarely opened room? They would not feel a chill if there were no fire there at all. Something very different it is, that makes their cheeks flush, and their necks show so deep a red.

The rest of the family go to bed earlier on Sunday night than on any other in the week; their plan is, to start fair and square with the next morning. One never hears of Blue Mondays among such people. If they must be thought blue at all, let it by all means be on the Sundays. On that night they wind their eight-day clocks, just like the old clock in Shandy Hall, — those tall, high-shouldered time-keepers that stand in square entries and upon so many broad stairs. The "meetin' clothes" of the children are laid away for another week, and the old ones got out again. Kindlings are split and piled ready to fire up on the morrow, and big armfuls of oak, and ash, and hickory, are placed handy to the hearth and stoves.

—— Upon the steady-going, industrious farmer of the North and East the influence of the recurring Sabbaths is incalculably good and lasting. If any one needs repose more than another, it is he. The mechanic of the large cities may rebuild his shattered energies with a jaunt up the river or down the bay; but even this sort of exhilaration has a far different quality from that which calms the nerves, cools the blood, and equalizes the spirits of the sober country farmer. On that one day, he pauses once more to *consider:* — wife and children about him, horses and cattle enjoying their rest, and he the head and lord of the whole domestic establishment, — he is almost conscious of being a patriarch in the land, and his character looms quite grand and columnar in the social landscape.

The fury and fuss of some Sundays elsewhere are in sharp enough contrast with one of these blessed Sabbaths in the country. From the still hour when the sun begins to redden the east, the whole roll of the hours is holy in the contemplation. All objects seem to be clothed in a special Sunday attire, — to look one in the face, as it were, and silently say, "It is Sunday." The people without exception dress themselves tidily and with peculiar care, from genuine respect for the Day itself. Children are held in wholesome, though often in rigid restraint, for the same reason. The very procession of the hours seems slow and solemn, and men's faces wear longer aspects, — not as deceitful masks at all, but only out of a decent and ingrained regard for the character and associations of the Day.

HUCKLEBERRYING.

I CANNOT help thinking that the boy who comes to manhood without knowing something of the simple and healthy pleasures of the Huckleberry Pasture, is hardly as sweet or whole a man for the unlucky omission. Because I believe in my heart that this same huckleberry field — like many simple gratifications that cost nothing and are little thought of at the time — is a real pasture-land for the spirit of the boy, whereon it feeds with an eagerness not paralleled by that of any of the experiences which come afterward.

Of the recurring delights of the summer-time, this one of huckleberrying assuredly belongs at the top of the list. It blossoms all over with the dearest associations, which have their countless fine roots in the very being; and these associations grow, too, along with the growth of the youthful heart. Neither circumstance nor years impair them; they only acquire a new freshness with the lapse of time.

——It is a secret pleasure of mine to sit and call up again, in musing mood, those happy days when a half dozen of us boys just out of school used to take our baskets and pails, and tramp off a couple of long and dusty miles over a country road for a summer day's huckleberrying. We were in the habit of foraging for this delicious wild fruit in some pastures that belonged to a kind and honest man — rest his soul! — who was known to us only as "Uncle Elisha." I well remember the easy gait we struck, when we came near the long and winding lane that led to the good man's little brown one-and-a-half story house, and the gay, childish snatches we shouted, rather than sang, as we trudged along the cart-path across the pastures on our way home again. The wide-spreading chestnut-tree down in the very bottom of the meadow bowl, stands out green and hospitably umbrageous before me now, its lowest limbs kindly holding for us the baskets and pails that carried our frugal dinners. Ah, what a matchless sauce was that which our voracious appetites supplied us with then! I see, too, the very bower by the roadside, made by the wild grape-vine that had seized hold of a promising young apple-tree and compelled it to stand still for the better display of its own leafy contortions; — the same vine next that moss-spattered stone wall, in whose sequestered shadows we all loved to huddle on our return home at sundown.

I remember just as well, too, how we used to lay the woolly mullein leaves over the glossy berries we had picked, and secure them with little twigs of the huckleberry bush, placed in the form of squares, and triangles, and octagons, and stars. The old bars to the pasture, of which there were two pairs, and the last of which, at the head of the lane, we had to climb, were a welcome landmark as we came trooping up out of the berry field; and, next to these, I may truly say, was the low roof of the house of "Uncle Elisha," and the well-sweep that always seemed to me to be poised in the air above it. Up along through that same old lane, our young feet trod a carpet whose like they will never walk over anywhere again; — Wiltons and Axminsters may not be named with that thick and verdant turf which received them with so soft a pressure, after the long day's tramping among the rocks, bushes, and brambles of the berry pasture. Occasionally, too, we used to get a drink of new milk at that same brown house; and it is very certain that, at such times, our industrious field-service was duly paraded before the eyes of the generous giver, basket after basket. Looking through the vista of memory to the figure of "Uncle Elisha's" wife, as she stood in that low back-door with a bumper of sweet milk for us in her hand, I can endorse every syllable the traveller Ledyard so truly says about Woman, and do it with an enthusiasm entirely unaffected.

—— There was still another field to which we rambled on these fragrant summer-day excursions. Three good miles distant was that, and to reach it we had to cross a long, covered toll-bridge. The little light that showed us our way across came in through the wide-apart and narrow windows cut, like loop-holes, in its sides, at which we used to stop and look down with a strange fascination into the swift current of the water. My conscience will never fully acquit me, I fear, of the guilt of having *run* that toll of a penny on many an occasion. The bridge was tended then by a brother of the revered and scholarly man, since gone to his heavenly rest, who afterwards turned me off his hands, declaring me fit for college. That occurred to me once as a strange coincidence somehow: in the haste and hubbub of this age of great things, the world would not think it worth naming. The lot itself, that lay a couple of long miles easterly from this bridge, went by the name of "Marsh Lot;" we used to speculate not a little among ourselves, why some people preferred to call it *mash* lot.

There was a story-and-a-half red house standing on the bleak knoll that commanded a view of it; and not a window, front or rear, but was "trimmed" with contrasting white paint. It is my purpose to go, some day, expressly to see if that bleak red house is yet standing; and then I *may* ramble again — but this time it will be without the old time companions — over the old huckleberry pasture, too, and suffer my heart to cry out, though in vain, for those it loved like its own self in those halcyon days of existence. I shall look up with wonder, no doubt, at trees which were spindling saplings then, and find low boughs, on which we used to hang our baskets and pails, now grown into the air above my head.

Since those days, Fortune has kindly led my feet into quite as pleasant paths elsewhere; where just as many berries grew, and just as much mullein abounded; and these new pastures have lacked nothing in the world to make them as dear to me as the old ones, save the fragrance of the boyish associations.

One of these stretches back just across a noisy little river with a pretty Indian name — The Natchaug: hemmed about, on the north and the south, with a thrifty growth of wood; of extremely irregular surface; and sloping, where it does not pitch, down to the rocky bed of the riotous stream.

Another lot there was — a distant pasture-land — which we reached after a good three-mile ride over any but smooth or level roads; high set and breezy; studded and bossed with old trees that stood far apart; and seamed with moist dells where the grass grew greener than anywhere else around. *One* day I certainly recall now, that went calmly by with me in this lonely huckleberry pasture, so sweet and pure in the light of a clear friendship, so full of the music of birds and wild bees, the bleating of sheep and low tinkle of cow-bells, that I often think earth and heaven must have kindly combined their influences, even some time before, to produce that particular day for my heart's everlasting remembrance.

—— It is as much an art to go a-huckleberrying as to make a sketch or a picture. In the first instance, one must feel himself in the right temper, since a spirit of inharmony spoils all, if it is allowed to get the upper hand; and that temper is to the last degree one of placidity and contemplativeness. You go straight to the wrong place, if you start for one of these nooks in Nature with a hot heart, or a fuming brain, and expect to meet with sympathizing circumstances. It is the last of places for unrest or ambition, if they go for any thing but more wretchedness.

The good home-folk take along baskets and birch-measures on their arms, and stroll leisurely off through lanes that are lined with the dense black alders, and down streaked cart-paths, and across patches of woodland, until they come face to face with the inevitable Bars; and by their moderate and almost indolent gait, one would suppose they dwelt in a realm where leisure was the law, and the highest energy of life was covered up with these abounding poetic similitudes. They walk with such an apparent freedom from all care, so that you would say their thoughts hung as heedlessly about them as their garments, that the whole landscape becomes peopled thereafter with the beautiful spiritual images which they excite.

All hands rendezvous at the Bars, the larger waiting for the little ones. This is the point of departure for all. Here the baskets and bark measures are distributed, each one taking what represents his expertness and industry as a berry-gatherer. The favored younglings assume each his or her allotted stent, and go their noisy way over or between the bars, to receive such impressions on their young hearts as will last them for a whole lifetime.

Generally, too, a few stray geese are to be seen straggling near the border wall, whose depredations on the fruit of the pastures are much greater than one who had not observed for himself would think possible. Or a pair of steady old oxen, turned out to graze and recruit, their necks relieved of the burdensome yoke, look up from their odorous bites in the yet dewy grass, as if they would ask what means this vociferous invasion. So early in the morning, a thrush is to be heard in the top of the birch hard by, caroling forth the joy his little breast knows not how to hold, and, it is like, offering all comers a gay welcome to the ecstasies of his own liberty. A singing sparrow, or perhaps a bustling little yellow-poll answers in the copse that hides the hill-side spring, and straightway the whole slope is a series of songful cascades.

Now they fall every one to his work, — for it is work indeed that they make of it, — and it is right here in the open air, canopied with the bare blue of heaven, the free summer winds playing ever so gently over the face, and the singing of birds and music of waters pouring their lulling current over the soul, that the berry-pickers chat as they work and work while they chat, fingers not a whit busier than tongues and both as busy as they can be, even their gay gossip becoming instantly purified in this most unworldly of all spots on earth, and, every hour, unconsciously drinking in those influences whose strength they cannot measure now, but which they will, at some other time, come to hold the most precious of all in their history.

Thus sprinkled over a berry pasture, a party of rustic pickers presents so striking a scene, the wonder is that no home artist, drawing inspiration from the very scents of our New England soil, ever thought to transfer it to his canvas and glorify it with the hues of his own imagination. It abounds with some of the most picturesque points to be found in the still home life of the country.

—— As fast as the little ones fill their measures, they trudge to the tree in whose shade are ranged their baskets and pails, and proceed with all deliberateness to "empty;" announcing, in shrill shouts, how full they have at this stage filled them. Gallants go off foraging, and come back with armfuls of broken bushes for the girls in the shade, with whom they sit down to pick and talk and frolic; and a marvellous lot of jolly chat it is, too, at these same little trees in the open huckleberry field. The heaps of withered bushes will surely betray these cosy gatherings under the trees to any one who finds and laments them, the summer after.

What a sweet and savory feast is the frugal lunch at noon! — eaten out in the air thus, and under trees that kindly catch and sprinkle down all the straggling breezes; washed down with water freshly fetched by the younger ones from the hill-side spring, that tastes of the cool earth out of whose bosom it was pressed. Even the delicious luncheons of the hay-field are surpassed for famous flavors and surrounding fragrance by this. At that hour, the day's stent has been advanced so far as to make it pretty clear what each one's performance is to be. They take this particular time to compare notes; and now the smartest picker — who is, of course, the stillest one, — receives the general praise without a thought of envy. The glossy black trophies in the basket are beautiful to feast the eyes upon; it does not seem possible that this rocky and brambly old pasture has yielded fruit in such abundance, and of flavors of such surpassing delicacy. By this time, likewise, all faces are well browned by the wind and sun of August, so that the little party seated under the hickory might be mistaken for a camp of strolling gypsies.

And afterward, as the long afternoon hours stretch on towards the sunset, what low and sad cadences of song fall on the sensitive hearing from little birds that domicil in the open pastures. One feathered throat perseveringly counsels all who take the trouble to listen, to "drink your tea — drink your tea!" — as if any possible decoction from over the seas could be better than the limpid drink brewed in the enclosure of this very home-lot! The harsh clangor of the geese, getting ready to take up their late afternoon march for a night on the bare ground under the corn-barn, strikes a different scale of associations; and the dull and regular stroke of the cow-bell, monotonous *campanile* that it is, another still; and yet a different one, the extempore warble of the robin in a wild cherry-tree near the wall; and yet another, the bark of a distant watch-dog, whose echoes seem to gather even a sort of melody, like the winding horn of the hunter, as they came circling across the still lake of the summer air. And all these sounds commingle mysteriously with other sounds, and again with one another, so that in such a place and at such an hour, the sensitive and contemplative soul lapses into a mood of the profoundest worship.

Trudging thoughtfully home again at nightfall, the sun throwing level beams across the landscape and lodging them in the tops of the trees, and the shadows deepening in the grassy lanes and damp lowland reaches, it rises in every one's thought that this one day out in the pastures has been the crown of all the days of the year. Not often does it indeed come round, whole and entire like this, in a single season; but still it holds its fixed place, like the sweet Pleiades in the heavens, in the calendar of every passing year.

Jaded and fagged, unable to go one step further, almost reeling and stumbling into the house, the excursionists finally bring in their berries and set them down on the table, and are ready for bed as soon as they have eaten their frugal supper.

Is there sweet sleep dispensed for the blessed anointing of mortal lids, by any of "the drowsy syrups of the world," like this which rests on the spirits of the tired huckleberry party?

Can even childhood throw itself into the arms of the drowsy god with a perfecter trust in his ability to bless with the single blessing it is too weary to ask for?

BARN LIFE.

IT is the man of the high latitudes chiefly, who strives to domesticate his sentiments and give them a genuine home expression. The inhabitant of Constantinople does not seek a like realization of his desires with the native of the Swiss Valley, or of the green slopes of English Kent. The dweller among the breezy New England hills nurses a very different sentiment concerning Home from his congener around the bayous of Louisiana, or more directly under the suns of the tropics. Hence the Northern house wears another aspect, and has entirely distinct belongings from that of any other latitude and location. The climatic needs being peculiar, the sentiment that springs out of them must, perforce, correspond.

May it not be accepted as an universal truth, that the love of Home exists nowhere, and is incapable of actual expression, except it is first caught wild from Nature, and shut down under ridge-poles and sheltering eaves and roofs? Is attachment to home best bred in caves and dens? Can Nomads be called home-loving? or Crowfeet and Flatheads know by experience of the domestic sentiments and virtues?

With the Home goes the Barn; that is a matter altogether of course. Hovels do not require barns as domestic complements; but Homes, with low roofs and broad hearths, do. The Barn is as much an object of interest as the dwelling, and the life that swarms and is sheltered in the one bears very close relationship to that which hives in the other. The good husbandman who fodders his sheep and cattle within the snug enclosures of his barn near home, grows more attached to them than if he merely knew they were browsing miles off in the woods, or straggling without aim across vast prairie lands, and here and there pulling at exposed hay-stacks. This love, too, becomes a personal affair, and, by its operation, the profounder love of locality and home is fixed and developed. If the man of New England migrates, it is only for better land and, therefore, a better HOME; but the man of Tennessee and Mississippi moves farther on, that he may own a thousand ACRES, in lieu of his present three hundred.

It is a fair study of the growth of sentiment

and taste, to look about the country and see how farmers place their barns; they may be estimated pretty well by so slight a token. I can go and put my hand on many and many a broad barn-door, that discloses an interior view pat before the home windows. Concerning the use and value of barns, their honest owners hold the right *idea*, but happen to be lamentably deficient in *taste;* and, no doubt, would frankly admit that they cared not a wisp of hay about it. They assume — what is true — that the barn is the workshop of the farm establishment, where all labor and profit begins and ends; and hence, like men who love their money-bags best of all things, they want the workshop where they can *see* it; and even permit the tyrannical sense of smell to become subordinate, where it should have its way unchallenged. Then, too, they would have their place of business as handy to the door as may be; like the shoemaker, with his plaything of a shop right in the L of his house, — or the doctor, whose instruments, jars, and saddle-bags lie kicking about like ordinary household trumpery.

There are two sorts of barns, now-a-days; the Commercial, and the Picturesque. Mechi, of London, writes overpoweringly of the former, with their famous plank floors and still more famous stall-feds, quite confusing you with the rattle of his estimates and figures; the latter are the barns — and the only ones, too — you will find in artists' landscapes, who study, not cent. per cent., but the most striking natural expression. It is these barns only, that deserve place in the landscape; it is these that children love to play in, on Saturday afternoons, and old men wander over with hands thoughtfully crossed behind them. These are the barns that rise to the imagination, on reading of Shakspeare's

> —— "rich leas
> Of wheat, rye, barley, vetches, oats and peas;
> Of turfy mountains, where live nibbling sheep,
> And flat meads, thatched with stover, them to keep."

These, where the bleat of young spring calves becomes musical, — and sly old hens hide up nests full of eggs, — and summer swallows twitter under the dark eaves in swarming colonies, — and the big doors swing in the wind with a rusty creak, so sad that it finally tempers itself in the heart to a real pleasure.

The commercial barns, the barns of mere business, with stately cupolas that screen principles of ventilation, — with paint, and blinds, and lightning-rod, and an equine vane, — elaborate with brand-new bins, and stalls, and pine-smelling floors, — such barns as these are not in pictures, are not of Homespun, are not the old brown barns that men and children love, and are sure to love as long as they live. Somehow, — though it is all natural enough, — our friends of the brush and palette catch the true hints and points; it must be on Falstaff's principle of "instinct": — and they are careful never to spoil canvas with either white barns or new ones. They go straight even to a dilapidated structure, with sagging doors and billowy roof, passing by such as merely cost and make money. Thus poverty has its charm, which must pass for one of its compensations; for poverty is ever picturesque in Nature.

I look about for barns that provoke most human sentiment, not those it took the most money to build. Such are the barns that go with the dwelling, and are not set off as objects for glancing admiration. Such as these are *not* the barns that are esteemed better than the houses their owners live in. These are low-roofed, and rambling. They abound with shelf-like scaffolds and irregular stairs, with cunning nooks and secreted shadows. They are primarily for service, like the men on whose shoulders the world rests; and therefore they are unpretending, and wear common clothes. In their warm shelter crowd Juno-eyed oxen, ruminant in the twilight of the place, or rustling fresh tumbles of the sweet hay. Their floors are broad, and have been soundly whipped with old-fashioned flails; and their bays are both deep and capacious. You can see the clear sky light pricking through the brown shingles, and sprinkling the whole hay-mow with its cerulean showers; as if it would fain follow the red-top and timothy even into their winter quarters.

I love to hunt hens'-nests in the hay, as well as the youngest child that can climb old stairs or straddle dizzy cross-beams and rafters. The clucking jades, with their strong family instinct, manage to discover the cosiest nooks and secretest corners, — now snug up against a big beam and now close beneath the eaves, under the thatch of a bundle of rye or cuddled in a fragrant cellar-hole of their own digging in the hay, — where they go every day to deposit the summer hopes of the yard, and afterward sit solitary and musing, waiting for the grass to sprout and the welcome peep of the new brood to make itself heard. It is "fun" to stumble upon these nests, for the whole household esteems them such prizes. A cap-full of freshly laid eggs, fetched into the kitchen without notice, creates a very general family joy. I do not believe the adventurer in El Dorado, who has fallen on a placer or struck suddenly upon a vein, feels a thrill of delight one whit more intense than the boy who, in the deserted old barn in the spring, comes upon the unexpected treasure of a nest-full of hens' eggs. Since Columbus broke *his* egg, in the shrewd and simple spirit of "Poor Richard," to discover and to find has been the delight of child and man, and probably will be to the end of human history. Discovery, in truth, is both the hint and pith of all development.

In these same dear old barns, too, the children are licensed to suspend swings, where the dreamy Saturday afternoons slip by almost unrecorded, but remain green memories ever after. What a multitudinous patter of little feet upon the oaken floor! What a riotous chorus of voices throughout the rambling old realm! What a musical tide of discordant noises, flowing out through the open doors over the yard! Now the prince of the ring sails up to the big beam, just touching it with the tips of his toes; and now he is tossed back to the very chinks that let in light so dimly under the eaves, or sweeps ever so airily across the uppermost scaffold, on this side, — and hangs, for a second or two, suspended over the yawning bay, on that. It is delightful, and indescribable; even the long sweep of the swing on the big elm near the house has no peculiar experience like this of the swing in the barn.

Spring starts new life in the barn and its precincts, just as in all other places. A very few days, steeped in the flood of its warming suns, are sufficient to empty all the stalls and send forth their occupants into the yards and the nigh pastures. The oxen alone come home at noon to bait, and timorous young calves lie with feet tucked under them in the deep pens, waiting for the coming of sundown and their milky mothers. Blue-frocked butchers may be seen scouring around the premises then, picking up what the winter may have added or left over. An old turkey slys in, with a winking eye and an open ear, to peck at stray seeds and keep the run of the capacious establishment; mayhap, considering if a snug home-nest somewhere hereabout may not, after all, be better than to take the chances of weather and foxes under the birches on the edge of the woodland.

In the yellow autumnal days, however, the

barn is in its real glory; for then it is full to bursting, and the farmer's hopes are at last garnered in. With hay packed and piled everywhere, crammed and crowded, overloading and overrunning, — with oats all threshed and winnowed, and poured into the bins and barrels, — with shocks of corn stacked away in all the corners and jogs and angles, encroaching on the floor, and allowing only narrow passages through to the cattle-stalls, — there broods within the barn a sentiment of snugness and warmth, to which few other sentiments are precisely comparable.

By scaling the hay-mow, in the middle of one of these same golden days, the sun falling through the open gable window across the hay, I have many a time lain and heard mice creeping about in their fragrant mines below, and childishly fancied them renewing former acquaintance in a spirit of frolicsome congratulation; as who should say — "Is not all this fixed up for us alone?" Or, again, I have caught the smothered voices of insects, exiles from foreign fields, that cling to the hay-stalks as the last hope of lengthening their little life of summer. They utter cries burdened with an indescribable melancholy, echoing in the heart unspoken presages of decay and death.

The various tribes are fairly represented here, — the same that colonized, in summer's greenness, on the hill-side slopes, and skimmed the thickly-standing spires of herd's-grass and foxtail, in the meadow. To lie thus on the sweet hay in autumn, and listen to these sounds in the spirit of interpretation, is to live over again, for only a sunny strip of days, the summer experiences in the meadow and beneath the trees that dot the green slopes of the upland. It is but the delicious summer lessons conned once more in the lap of autumn, with all the sounds and scents of summer to impress them on the sensitive memory.

When the great doors are shut, at evening, and the lantern hangs from the beam overhead, and a happy group of men and boys sit and husk the yellow corn about the middle of the floor, and the round moon hangs luminous in the autumn sky, — the chickens all snug on their roosts in the apple-trees, and the turkeys poised for the night on heights even above them, — no Arab tent or gypsy encampment ever offered more striking points of real picturesqueness; the added charm of the corn-husking scene comes from its domestic associations, which the other pictures lack. The old farmers stint themselves to so many ears, of an evening; and they will relate their exploits years afterward, when the topic comes up for friendly brag and comparison. The young people, in particular, set great store by these times; for there are slyer chances for a kiss, up here in the half-shadows, than were ever to be found at all the bees and quiltings; and "gracious knows" how many tender passages have shaped and fixed whole human lives afterward!

The thumping flails, through these sunny and contemplative days, answer one another from farm to farm across the valleys, beating tattoo for the welcome harvest-time. They sound dull or ringing, on the hills and in the valleys, as the wind breezes from or toward you. Like the loud tickings of the tall clock in the house, they notch off the bushels of glossy grain that are to be slipped into the granary.

And when Winter has set in with serious intent, one can enjoy hours in the barn even then, adding insensibly to the stores of his contemplation. It is pleasant to see the cattle feeding in their stalls, after being all well housed and bedded for the night. They hardly look at you now, their moist muzzles so masked with wisps of sweet fodder; but their thick necks, –

—— "whose throats have hanging at tnem
Wallets of flesh," —

their branching horns, their broad shoulders and brawny backs attract you, in spite of yourself; and you stay only to grow glad, as a child would, in thinking of their winter comforts and plenty, after a season of such pleasant summer days off in the turfy pastures.

As I have already observed, the Barn seems to be the farmer's Study, where he thinks his thoughts, gathers together his hints, and learns practically all his lessons; and I have undertaken to illustrate a part of this fancy with some simple verses, that may be none the better or worse for that singular quality: —

UP IN THE BARN.

Old Farmer Joe steps through the doors,
  As wide to him as gates of Thebes;
And, thoughtful, walks about the floors
Whereon are piled his winter stores,
  And counts the profits of his glebes.

Ten tons of timothy up there,
  And four of clover in the bay;
Red-top that cut — well, *middlin'* fair,
And bins of roots, oblong and square,
  To help eke out the crop of hay.

A dozen head of cattle stand
  Reflective in the leaf-strewn yard;
And stalks are stacked on every hand,
The latest offering of the land
  To labor long maintained and hard.

Cart-loads of pumpkins yonder lie —
  The horse is feeding in his stall —
The oats are bundled scaffold high,
And peas and beans are heaped hard by,
  As if it were some festival.

At length old Farmer Joe sits down, —
  A patch across each of his knees;
He crowds his hat back on his crown,
Then clasps his hands, — so hard and brown, —
  And, like a farmer, takes his ease.

"How fast the years do go!" says he;
  "It seems, in fact, but yesterday,
That in this very barn we three —
David, Ezekiel, and me, —
  Pitched in the summer loads of hay!

"David, — he sails his clippers now;
  And 'Zekiel died in Mexico; —
Some one must stay and ride to plow,
Get up the horse, and milk a cow, —
  And who, of course, but little Joe?

"I *might* have been — I can't tell what! —
Who knows about it till he tries? —
I *might* have settled in some spot
Where money is more easy got;
Perhaps beneath Pacific skies.

"I *might* have preached, like Parson Duer;
Or got a livin' at the law;
I might have gone to Congress, *sure;*
I might have kept a Water Cure;
I *might* have gone and been — oh, pshaw!

"For better far it is as 't is;
What fortune waits him, no man knows;
What he has *got*, that, *sure*, is his;
It makes no odds if stocks *have* riz,
Or politicians come to blows!

"Content is rich, and somethin' more —
I think I 've heerd somebody says;
If 't ever rains, it 's apt to pour;
And I am *rich*, on this barn floor,
When all is mine that I can raise!

"I 've plowed and mowed this dear old farm
Till not a rod but what I know;
I 've kept the Old Folks snug and warm,
And lived without a twinge of harm, —
I don't care how the storm might blow.

"And on this same old farm I 'll *stay*,
  And raise my cattle and my corn;
Here shall these hairs turn wholly gray;
These feet shall never learn to stray;—
  But *I will die where I was born!*"

And Farmer Joe pulled down his hat,
  And stood up on his feet once more;
He would not argue, after that,
But, like a born aristocrat,
  Kept on his walk about the floor.

A MORNING AT THE BROOK.

HOW much comes of association; and that is the delicious fruit of observation, of temperament, and of time. A brook is, of itself, an idle little thing; yet it possesses very varied combinations of power, after it has once found its way through a susceptible heart. A tree stands out statuesquely in the landscape, — simply a tree, with head, stem, leaves, and branches. But we fall into a pleasant habit of sitting in its shadow, and of silently telling over the stories of our sorrows and joys, of our desires and disappointments to the green thatch it builds above our heads, — and from that day this tree becomes a friend, a confidant, and, in truth, a part of our very selves.

—— Out of the twelve months of the year, June and October are our especial favorites. Perhaps October is fuller of what are really deep delights, the atmosphere then having an infusion — as the skyey cope has a coloring, — of that genuinely spiritual quality which rains down for the soul the true manna of nourishment. The sights and sounds of delicious June are possibly more sensuous than those of dreamy October; the earth, the sky, waters, birds, trees, buds, — all are expressive of the emphasis of promise; and that presents its appeal to the heart through the senses, making it leap up at last, in its very overplus of joy. But Nature is especially given to contrasts; thus she produces her finest effects. June being so wholly distinct from October, its very name reading like a poem in the calendar, it might be expected that the experiences it brings freshly every year might be distinct also.

June is the eastern, as October is the western gate of the Year. She trips in across a carpet of brightest verdure, the posts and pillars and arch at the entrance clustered with vines and burdened with roses. She goes out in majestic pomp and state, canopied with skies that reflect dazzling hues, the cool green transmuted now to scarlet and purple, orange and gold. Yet, June does but throw October into brighter and more beautiful relief. Each makes a fine foil for the other. And, for ourselves, having so long been in the habit of coupling these heavenly months, it never falls to our fortune to enjoy the one without thinking of the other also. In our heart, they were always twinned. Their names alone are like boxes that are compacted with the fragrance of peculiar delights. It is needless for us moderns to hope to surpass the underrated ancients in the bestowal of nomenclatures that are indeed poetic.

—— A June morning was newly born to us not many months ago, of which we feel very certain that we had dreams beforehand, for many a year. It is true, we had drunk the breath of many a June morning in its beauty, but of none before like this. It was ours, the moment it dawned, and as such it was instinctively laid hold of. So, indeed, do all things in nature belong to us, if we could but trace the divine right of possession and use.

We awoke with the low trill of the earliest bird — the song of a tawny-breasted robin, whose little heart was swelling with love for its household treasures in a tree hard by. With that first gush of song our soul came to life again. While the morning's gray still enveloped everything out of doors, and the rustic household continued its sleep of an innocent care, we made haste to put on our daily attire, and crept silently down the stairs and through the passages. Hastily disposing of a cold bite, and swallowing a draught of sweet "night's milk" with the cream clotting the surface, we pocketed the well-scoured angle-dogs, shouldered our birch fishing-rod, and sallied forth for a little thread of a brook whose every wayward twist and turn had long been perfectly familiar.

It cost a tramp of a mile or more. The dust in the country road lay a little matted under the dews, while, as we trudged on, we caught the ever welcome sound of cattle lowing in the pastures, on this side and the other, impatient for the return of companions that were yarded the night before. There was not the lightest breath of a breeze astir. Now and then, an early bird flitted across from one roadside covert to another, offering us the welcome of a true fellowship with a quick chirp and the flirt of a brown wing. The dappled east was rapidly becoming glorified with the colors that were beginning to pile themselves in such splendid disarray. As we pushed on up the road, more solitary in thought than if the hour were that of midnight, it very forcibly occurred to us how much they were the losers who never left their beds out of the accustomed hours. Here was a little fresh morning jaunt, now, worth a good many times the trouble it cost, for it took us almost insensibly into the realm of new experiences.

We scaled some mossy bars, ranged off down a slope among a few stunted apple-trees, and, to be brief, were not long in reaching the brookside. Close by was a strip of woods; into which we plunged for a few minutes only, that no possible impression of the morning might be lost upon us. In that cool twilight which seemed braided by bough and leaf, the bird family were just getting up and coming down from their airy chambers. They called gayly one to another from out the windows of their different apartments, as if asking of the new morning that re-created the world for them; and their piping voices echoed through every sylvan arch and along every leafy corridor. The green and velvety mosses under foot were scarcely damp, and the short grasses hardly held a pearl on the points of all their blades, such complete protection the dense umbrage offered against the night dews.

In the heart of the morning silence — which is an awakening rather than a dreaming silence — we were startled by the noise of young cattle roving through the wood, breaking down the tender undergrowth of shrub and brush, and half-boldly, half-timidly advancing within eye-shot of so unfamiliar an intruder. Their wild eyes, answering to the Homeric epithet, were as full of lustre as the beads of dew that Night had scattered over the grass of the meadow.

Emerging from this verdurous temple, and leaving the happy birds behind us, we crept stealthily down to the edge of the wimpling stream, and made the first cast of the morning. The brook, where we stood, was scarcely bigger than our body, — which we cannot in conscience assert has not waxed somewhat since that day; and the shy little Naiad seemed trying to hide itself among the sedges and under the long, rushy grasses. We stood knee-deep now in the wet and matted jungle of the morning, while all around us, in among the slender stems of the grass, insects without name or number were just starting up to enjoy the gay sport of their span-long summer existence. And while in this half-surprised posture, up came the flaming sun over the eastern hills, and began pouring its golden glory like a flood into the sparkling basin of the meadow.

As we tramped along, making a fresh cast

of the line with every few steps, and leaving but a single trail in the heavy grass behind us, each advance revealed to the delighted eye newer and expanded charms. Now the spirit took in the meaning of the freshness and sweet fragrance of Morning. Snatches from the rural poets came singing their way into our heart, like golden-zoned bees driving homeward with their freights of honey. Over night, the busy spiders, with the instinct of Penelope, had spun slenderest ropes of very gossamer, and swung them across from one grass-spire to another, each rope, like a suspension bridge, heavy with its string of pearly dews, which the fancy delighted to believe early passengers.

We frightened a callow bird out of his hiding-place among the tussocks, where he was squatted with upturned bill, waiting in dumb patience for the coming of his provident mother. A lithe and string-like black snake uncoiled himself from the fork of an alder-bush, and slid down with a slump, that is in our ears now, into the water. The homely chewink advertised us of her brisk whereabouts, by her musical monotone in the neighboring thicket of birches. A gay little yellow-poll played an eager air on his bagpipe, as if he would frankly ask us how we liked *that*, so bright and early in the morning. The polyglottal bobolink careered in a sort of drunken delight across the level stretch of meadow, and alighted on a frail rush stem at last, to *swing* out the rest of the little joy he had not strength to *sing*.

By and by, the voices of boys could be heard over on the opposite hill-sides, screaming their shrill " Go-long! " to cows that were too slow for their temper. Next, the hissing sound of scythes, grinding for the morning's work down in the mowing. Then a cart, rattling with a great noise over a stony length of the road. And now, cattle lowing to one another from all the hill-sides, — and young calves bleating, — and the whole day fairly awake with its sounds of life and activity. Still, along down through the meadow we pursued our devious way, casting and recasting our line in the water, twisting our path just as the little brook twisted its own course, — errant and tortuous, — that kept whispering and smiling, prattling and laughing to us, till we ached to know of what pleasant secret the sprite would wish to unburden itself to our ears.

—— How many speckled beauties were ours, as a tribute from the little brook that morning, a peep into our creel would have readily disclosed; but we found finer things to feed on than trouts in that charmed spot, greatly as we admire and love even them.

Such a morning, three good hours long as we made it, lies in my memory now like the fresh picture of a world of which we feel that, in some previous existence, perhaps, we may once have dreamed. It was every whit itself. Nothing else could be like it. It would be styled a very cheap pleasure by many, because there was no carriage hire needed to reach it; but such are the only pleasures, let us remember, that are afterwards called up as the green spots of the lifetime. Nothing of this sort can be found up for sale. Money bears no relation to it. High health, deep lungs, an open eye, ready perceptions, and a fresh and innocent heart, — these are all the few and simple conditions.

And yet the world hurries to Newport and the Springs for *pleasure*, and is bored to death with the delights it enjoys in such surfeit! A little idle brook, romping out of the alder thickets and stealing down through the open meadows, shall, for true tranquility and genuine satisfaction, put all their artifices to shame. We never turn away our face from the brookside and start homewards, without repeating the exquisite lines quoted by gentle Izaak Walton and credited by the Father of Angling to Sir Henry Wotton : —

> "May pure contents
> Forever pitch their tents
> Upon these downs, these meads, these rocks, these mountains;
> And peace still slumber by these purling fountains,
> Which we may every year
> Meet when we come a-fishing here."

OUR AUNT.

SHE was just seventy when she died; but we never seemed to think, till then, of her being any older than on the day she was forty. She inherited youth to a most generous degree:—the new morning was not more fresh than the flow of her spirits.

Most people associate Aunts with sharp-edged words, and phrases that might have been run in an iron mould; with suspicious supervision, two wrinkles between the eyes, and a voice from which drop the distillations of anything but honey. Addison describes them, in one of the numbers of the "Spectator," as "antiquated Sybils, that forebode and prophesy from one end of the year to the other;" and in too many cases they are quite content to answer to the description. It would outrage my feelings beyond account, however, to compare *our* Aunt with the common run of Aunts who may be catalogued under one or the other of the foregoing descriptions.

She was a great lover of Nature's own things. The stay-behind robins knew at whose door they could get free board — with lodgings about the barn and sheds — through the weary, dreary winter; and the woodpeckers and snow-birds understood, with no further telling, that the meaty bones, hung at the back of the house, were exclusively for their picking. Children were not more alive, in the dawn of the June mornings, to catch the earliest note of the three o'clock robin, or to find their round nests-full of eggs snugged away under the leaves. So fresh a heart is childhood's own; but she had it, and she kept it, too, up to the day she became three-score and ten. For even while she lay, one April afternoon, on the bed on which she shortly after died, she lifted her head to greet, as she would a personal friend, the pretty blue jay that flew to the low roof close by and tried to look in at her window. — It was a touch of nature that started tears in the eyes that witnessed such simplicity of affection.

Among the children, while they were coming on and coming up, she was esteemed almost like an own mother. They never felt a twinge of fear in her presence, but rather sought the magnetism of her smiles and the glad contagion of her humor. She was young once more with *them;* and as they grew in years and in wisdom, she managed, with the help of her warm and ready sympathies, to keep pace with them, too. It was all very beautiful; I take it upon me to say that no other family group ever furnished an Aunt in this respect the parallel of ours.

An Aunt is too apt to be a sort of nightmare in a house; children conceal everything they can from her: — but *our* Aunt was made a repository of all the precious secrets there were on foot. She gave us counsel and made us fun. Her dignity was imbedded in her character, not pinned on to the surface of her gown, or starched into the high crown of her cap. For childish low spirits or moodiness she was an all-cure. She never shed tears, and would not revive sorrows. Her whole life was in *living*, not in a vague hope that she would do so after present troubles were past. Every anecdote that had currency in her own youth she gayly reproduced for the illustration of ours; every odd phrase she could call up from the recollections of a generation that went before ours, she passed around in our little circle like good coin that had been clipped. Her own school-days were somehow made to fit into our school-days; the beaux of her time found their reproduction in the gallants of ours; she never tired of repeating the unique sayings of her earlier days, nor did we of listening to her. She turned every accident humorously, and so taught us by example how to defy disappointment. If things had gone wrong heretofore, they were sure to come right by and by. Hopefulness was as generously hers as mirth; and both combined to form a third quality of cheerfulness that made sunshine around her in the cloudiest day.

And maiden aunt though she was, no one ever felt her to be one of those "proper" bodies whose presence seems to make the atmosphere thick and heavy. There was no taint of judicial severity about *her;* she enjoyed far too much to let it effervesce or waste in criticism. She had been gifted with such generous store of genuine sentiment or sympathy, it was no office of hers to be following up others with the everlasting line and plummet. Those who have been wont to run *from* maiden aunts would assuredly have run *toward her.* Cheerfulness in persons of ripened years is always attractive and charming; but in her, even mirth was peculiarly becoming. None had a heartier relish of innocent laughter than she; and she was a practised hand in the art of provoking it besides. Saintly and affectionate as she was at heart, and simple and sweet as her nature was all the way through, there was no lack, either, of the fine clay of earthliness which makes of our ideal delights a present reality. If she knew what affection was worth, and how to bestow it, too, she likewise understood what a genial stimulant it always found in a bright fire, a warm room, and an attractively spread table. She believed in the substantials, while her heart was none the less open to the wavering, floating dreams of the invisible.

I realize now what a comfort it used to be to her, — and what a blessed memory it will always remain to me, — for me to sit with her in her chamber, of quiet Sunday afternoons, and read aloud her favorite chapters and passages in the old Bible that always lay on the little stand in the corner. The sublime simplicity of Job affected her; I knew that she was conscious of the temporary rapture of feeling, equally with him who sat and read on. Her charity and long-suffering were truly beyond description's reach; she was patient and forgiving when many of us would indeed lose our own patience for her. We never heard murmurs from her lips; she of course had disappointments, like the rest of us, but she had no complaint to make of them; neither, on the other hand, was she entirely indifferent to the turns and changes of fortune; — but a spirit of repining never could find a place to build its nest in that happy heart. Whoever sorrowed and lamented in her presence, found but poor companionship.

—— How shall I write of her spinning-wheel — an heir-loom in the family — which she kept buzzing every winter until the last one of her life, though the days of hand-spinning were long ago over? She averred that she spun merely to perpetuate the good old custom. The old wheel stood in the attic, and there, weather permitting, she went off alone with her rolls of white wool, and presently made the rafters vibrate with its droning music. We used to go softly to the stairs, and listen to her as she kept up singing and spinning together; — nobody would have said that house lacked for a light heart then. — The Past must have vividly reproduced itself in this chosen solitariness of hers, and father, mother, and grandparents must have seemed to make their appearance almost with the starting of the wheel.

I never came home from a tramp along the brookside for trout, but she displayed all the eagerness of a child to know my luck; and she would stand and contemplate the spotted beauties as I drew them forth from my basket, with a satisfaction almost the parallel of my own. And whatever trophies I brought to the house from the swamps or hill-sides, or from the berry pastures — whether wild flowers, or pretty birds'-nests which I had found deserted, or baskets of glossy berries — got as earnest a welcome at her hands as if she were young along with me, and only regretted that she, too, could not be out of doors through all the pleasant weather. My own field stories she matched with hers; and she betrayed as close and patient observation of life in the meadows and along the edge of the hill-sides as if she were a born naturalist.

Whenever she went idly scouting across the soft turf of the orchard, or the mowing, or the pasture, she invariably carried in her hand a long stick, partly for support, but chiefly to poke about and hunt up with; that stick was thrust into every hiding-place where it was thought a guinea's nest might be laid away; kindly helped her across the moist places and glistening little runnels; raked away the leaves from the brown chestnuts that were rained down in autumn; and was at last laid on the wall, or stood against the back shed, when she reached the door of Home again.

It was a passion with her to raise turkeys; and inasmuch as the sly old jades loved to roam off into the edge of the woods back of the house, I am grateful for being permitted to remember the times I have beaten up those woods for her, beginning pretty early in March, to solve the problem of her turkeys' prolonged absence. She had as anxious and tender a care for the young poults, after they broke the shell, as if they had been her very children; fetching them into the house over night — the weaklings among them — and nursing and coddling them up with such various preparations as the lives of so many generations of turkeys have depended upon. Just before bedtime, it was slightly amusing to go out into the kitchen and "stir up" her feathered hospital near the stove, or on the warmed hearth. In her thoughts, the spring was associated with the coming off of hens with their downy broods, just as much as with the sprouting of cowslips and dandelions. No poet ever wove tenderer sentiments on that joyful season into the staple of his verse.

Few came to the house to stay, who had not thought beforehand as much of enjoying the company of our Aunt as of the best of us.

And in calling up pleasant reminiscences of their visits, long afterward, her name rose almost the first of all on their lips. The house was much the sunnier because of her presence. She could not bear trouble, but preferred to drive it off with laughter and light-heartedness. I did not touch the depth of her philosophy then; but I see now how much she gained, and everybody else can gain, by refusing hospitality to thoughts of trouble and bolting the door of the heart against the messengers of low spirits. She wasted no part of her life in standing and parleying with these dismal shadows. Where she was, we were sure to find bright skies. The influence of such a person over a family of children, when exerted day by day for a regular course of years, while the plastic nature is receiving the most delicate impressions, can hardly be put into expression, for it can be estimated only through the term of a whole life.

—— We stood about her open grave on a soft day in April, which seemed, with two or three kindred days, to have been slipped into the calendar of our uncertain springs, as Nature's own gentle tribute to her memory. Not all the praises of the world, had they been recited for her sainted name then, could have been so welcome and so precious to us as this bright and open favor which was silently dropped out of the blue skies. The grass was starting along the country roadsides, and its shades of green showed daintily up the slopes. The meadows just over the stone walls were moist with the spring rains, and the rivulets glistened in the distance with laughing gladness at their release. The beautiful day was so like her own spirit; sunny, cheerful, and calm. Our sadness received a sharper edge for so obvious an association.

—— I shall never pluck the wild flowers of spring by the woodside again, but my thoughts will go straight to her. I shall not wander in the huckleberry pastures and gather handfuls of the glossy fruit she loved herself to pick, without feeling her very presence. Up in the attic, I shall always seem to hear her voice. When we all assemble again in the old rooms of Home, it will not be as it used to be, without her. It is the blessing of a life to have had such a good soul to love. Childhood is so much the richer for it, and the after years are penetrated with the influence to their end.

AUTUMN DAYS.

ON him who goes forth into the woods and fields during these ripe autumnal days, in a spirit suffused with gentleness, and peace, and all the harmonies of the time, there descends an influence that makes the face of Nature into a new picture, and draws from it an expression which the heart loves to brood upon in the sweet silence of contemplation.

The spell is a strange one that works with such potency through the placid passage of these golden days, eluding analysis or explanation. So gauzy is the airiness with which the halo veils woods and waters, meadow and hillside, that it at length comes to envelop the sympathetic spirit's self in its welcome folds, and discovers to the penetrating vision dreams which are of rest, and bliss, and heaven.

How many are the enticements which present themselves out-doors, at this time! There is too much heat, and a feeling of lassitude, in the daily development of Spring; but *now*, all is so cool and tranquil, — the pastures lie so still in the lap of the haze, — the sun's heat is so gentle and genial, — the atmosphere bathes the spirit in so deliciously indolent a current, — that it is a delight just to be out doing little but breathing, letting the eyes wander idly this way and that, and silently answering with the spirit to the calls that may be heard by the sensitive ear all over God's perfect creation.

—— An Autumn Day has neither heat nor haste in it. It is a perfect thing. Like the Ethiop's pearl, it seems to lie dissolving its little riches in the vast beaker whose rim is the horizon. Placidity utters itself through all its quiet expression. Contemplation — that slow and sure ripening process of the human soul — steeps itself in its delicious atmosphere. We instinctively suffer our feet to lead us off among the trees, and develop a new love for being alone. Solitudes are delightful now, because they supply their own companionship. Nature's self is enough, and more than enough. We would ask for nothing, for life now is deep and full.

Instead of the ruddy apple-blossoms of May down in the orchard, we have the trees heavy with the thick globes of polished fruit. All the bars between the pastures are down, and the cattle may stray where they will. The brown stubble harbors armies of sable crickets, that skip away in rows before approaching feet. The hill-sides begin to look faded and a little sere, the wild-grape vines on the ledges turning brown and yellow, and the brakes parting with their juicy greenness. That beautiful American heath plant — the whortleberry bush — now shows ruddy, or russet red; and the sunshine nestles in its masses with a look of melancholy that is like a speechless lamentation for the lost delights of the summer. The choke-berries, in their long and clustering spikes, display red, or black, as they bend down their supporting stems; and flocks of tawny-breasted robins gather everywhere about the sunny ledges where they grow, discussing their journey southward into genial winter quarters.

You will see, on nearing the skirts of the woodland, busy squirrels racing in and out on the riders of the rail fences, their cheeks stuffed out with stolen corn. A clumsy woodchuck, fat from his autumnal foraging on the farmers' pumpkins, trundles off across the patch of ploughed land over the wall, afraid lest the dogs have spied and will bring him to stern account before he can quite whisk his gray tail into his domicil. Who would seriously care to revel in the sweet abundance with which he gorges himself, if every sound is charged with fear, and his heart beats with sudden suggestions of apoplexy?

At home, in and around the house, these days are like no other. All about the yard and garden, it is almost religiously still. A voice makes a circle in the air, like a stone dropped in a lake. The overgrown chickens wallow, in lazy luxury, under the currant-bushes, having discarded scratching altogether. The wasps swarm around the chamber and attic windows, stealing in with every chance, and colonizing in such warm and secret nooks as handily offer themselves. The garden vegetables, if not got in, are ripe to their utmost fulness; and the wilted vines and haulms lie decaying over the spots where but yesterday they erected columns and spires of freshest verdure. It is a more than half sad feeling that rises in the heart now, as one opens the little garden-gate and strolls down the central walk to the summer-house; not quite of sorrow, nor of regret that all the green pomp of summer is gone; but a tender and delicious grief, such as one would not avoid, that seems to flow out of the very sun and air into the receptive soul. And that is just the secret; we are in closer harmony with earth and its mysterious influences, at this season, and disposed, like little children, to throw ourselves upon her charitable love and into her open arms. This autumnal magnetism works purgatively on the whole year's spiritual humors, expelling what is incapable of assimilation with our natures, and, by holding us half asleep and dreamy in the adyta of earth's quietude, bringing us into more intimate and holy relations with ourselves than we were conscious of before. In this regard, the Autumn days are indescribably peculiar; the soul runs over with happiness, and we know it for a truer and purer happiness because it has no impetuosity, no superficial heat or hurry, but rather an undertone of sadness that cannot be forced to the surface in language.

If I were compelled to give up all but one particular portion of the year, this should be the one I would cling to longest. Because these are, of all the others, the most truly *divine days* in the calendar; fuller of spiritual meaning and spiritual delight. These invite contemplation more than the others; fill all the respiratory organs of the soul with the oxygen of their calm purity; are peopled with more visions of genuine imaginative beauty; and are more clear of those films and cloudy screens that at other times overcast the spirit's canopy. They take us to heights in the landscape of life where we get larger views than before. They sober our impulses, calm our restlessness, hold us with a gentle firmness to our own proper plane, establish the centripetal force within us, and develop a personal insight that stands forth first in the order of the soul's faculties. If they have not a brook-like torrent of joy dashing and foaming through them, like some few other days of the year, they are, nevertheless, seamed and grooved deeply with those streams that run by silently, and with accumulated power.

Nature calls to us, every one, — "Come out! come out! and let us know one another better!" One *feels* the expression and the emphasis of the call, when one goes thoughtfully skirting the rustling cornfields, thick with the yellow ears, or passes devoutly within the illuminated temple of the woods, glorified with the combined colors of the year. Even the semicircular army of turkeys, ranging the pastures for the skipping fatlings of the grass, seem as much a part of the scene, and their low, melancholy cry is as much a real voice of the time, as the skies and the woods and the hazy smoke themselves. The cows that graze along the hill-sides are of contemplative mien, and look mildly up at you, thus disturbing their solitudes, as if they would fain inquire whether you be of their way or no. And all among the shy little coverts, where was the dark secrecy of green leaves through early summer, is now reflected the bright light of hanging cloths of russet and crimson and gold. The wild creeper on the stone wall has been dipped in the dyes of the transmuting atmosphere, and come out a frill of brilliancy that makes the old wall regal in the memory afterward.

How gayly chatters that rascally red squirrel overhead, about affairs at home, including his prospects for the winter! As who should say to the crafty woodsman, skulking with gun and dog to surprise him, — "Sir, be content, if you please, to live and let live! You would be in better business if you would go in quest of bigger game!" The pond is mottled with the painted autumn leaves, which it slowly drags down, at last, to "muddy death," paving its broad floor with the same gay mosaic it has so recently reflected in its surface. A covey of plump quails start up from under the rail fence, making a whistling thunder with their wings that almost stops the beating of your heart. No song-birds are caroling their hymns now, but even they appear to have drawn into their little breasts the peculiar thoughtfulness of the air. They flit by, from spot to spot; but it is in silence, for they are packing up for lower latitudes.

All sounds and voices now are freighted with another meaning. The cawing of sable flocks of crows in the woods, — the bleat of sheep in the far pastures, — the shout of boys to the toiling oxen in the cornfield, — the lowing of cattle across the distant hills, — the sharp, quick bark of the watch-dog, or the eager hunter, in the wood patch, — the noisy cackling of hens about the barn, — reach the ear on so subdued and sweet a key, that one cannot but wish he might feel the waves of so soft a medium beating about him through all the year, preserving the poetic qualities of sound as perfectly as flies are preserved in amber. The laughter of the children, nutting in the grove of hickories and chestnuts, is like no other laughter heard; no atmosphere but this could so fix its delicious qualities in the ear and heart.

And when the sunset hour approaches, and the great god of light prepares to gather about him the yellow folds of haze and mist, and the whole air holds such a "solemn stillness" that one can almost talk with his thoughts aloud, the lonely katydid shrilling her hoarse cry up in the chambers of the elms and sycamores, and the crickets chiming in with their melancholy refrain in the matted grass and faded stubble, — then the hush is so complete that the heart acknowledges the spell laid upon it; the soul involuntarily assumes the attitude of prayer; and the experience that is born of the hour, silent and profound as it is, makes a close to the day as fitting as it is spiritually memorable. No man may yield himself to these influences, and say, in his heart, he is not both more and better than he was before. He secretly confesses — if he is wont to watch the silent processes of his own growth — that, with the days, he ripens, too; and that, along with the season, he may become more and more glorious to the end. This is no more, then, the year's autumnal time than it is our own; in its broad lap all the sheaves and hopes are heaped and pressed down.

—— Ah, how we are carried back — far back, sitting and thinking of the yellow suns lying up against the side of the brown barn, — of the pumpkins piled on the rough oaken floor, — of the flock of turkeys crowding in the yard at sunset, — and of the little ones just come home from the woods, scratched, and worn, and weary, and good for nothing more except bread-and-milk for supper and a soft bed under the roof! Who does not like to sit down and live the past over again? Who feels so sure of having got all there is to be had from these days and nights, — these mornings, and afternoons, and moonlit evenings, — that he does not care to go back once more, and glean for a little while after his earlier and briefer experiences?

THANKSGIVING.

SNOW used to fall, in years gone by, a day or two before Thanksgiving. There was always a great deal of bustle in the city markets, as also in the village stores and out among the farms. It is *at Home*, however, where the genuine interest culminates, rather than about the city stalls or within the country stores.

On the *very* day before this fine old festival, they are up betimes at the Homestead, foddering the cattle and feeding the poultry, while the various chores, nameless for number, are looked after as they should be. Every individual feels an individual responsibility. Word has come, in good season, of the proposed return to the old hearth of the entire list of brothers and sisters, sons and daughters, together with the retinue of wives, husbands, and children. 'The District School has not "kept" since the week began, that the field might be quite clear of impediments to family enjoyment. The master has gone home, as well as others. The village stores are filled with fresh barrels of flour, and boxes of new spices, and piles of turkeys, geese, and chickens, in every vacant spot where they may lie. Here and there, against the dingy walls, hangs a brace of partridges, trapped by some skulking fellow who passes more than half his time roving in the woods; or a solitary gray rabbit, brought in as a strictly personal speculation.

Soon enough after breakfast, work begins in earnest. There are children in plenty all about the poultry-yards to witness and assist at the general slaughter. Turkeys are singled out for the block, and die "without a sign." Chickens follow in fateful order close after. There is an indiscriminate spirting of fresh blood all around the chop-log, a great flutter of feathers and headless hornpipes over the scattered chips, and the annual door-yard butchery is over. While, within the house, Industry has suddenly raised itself to the place of a tyrant. Everybody is busy, — is at work. The carcasses of fowls are getting plucked in a darkened back-room. Only the aged people sit idly complacent at the fireside, chatting of their fears about the weather and the coming home again of the children, during the day.

The kitchen is a sort of household mart, in which things great and small are each in its turn attended to. Hurry and bustle, though without actual confusion. Long tables and square tables, and small stands in the corners. Flour and dough, and plates and pans. So many sleeves rolled up, so many white arms made whiter with flour dust. Such pleasant South Sea smells of spices, and such clouds of irresistible steams and odors. So many big and little wooden trays, and round plates, — white, with blue edges. And spoons, and knives, and rolling-pins, and flour-dredgers. Delf trays, likewise, filled nearly full with mince-meat for the pies, long seasoned and moistened, with a wooden spoon sticking up. And large pans of stewed pumpkin, strained through sieves, and colored richly with milk that blankets itself, every night, with cream. And dishes of cranberry, all prepared for its deft transmutation into tarts. And pans of apple-sauce, too, ready at hand for the pastry covers that are in process of making.

By noon, or certainly within three hours after, the uncles and aunts begin to flock in, as doves come back to the olden windows. Sons and daughters along with them, too, running over with joy to get back to the home of

Grandpa and Grandma. The old halls and passages ring with glad exclamations. Youthful voices and older ones intermingle, like gold and silver threads twisted together. A farmer son; a merchant son; a daughter, with a professional husband; a bachelor son, the odd one of the family lot: — all return gladly, and feel it a religious duty to come back to this time-hallowed festival, and receive once again the old folks' blessing. A sort of "picked-up" dinner is set before them, which, perforce, must answer till the cheerful meal at evening.

Than this no pleasanter picture of the old style of domestic happiness is to be painted on any imagination. One son strolls about the premises, inspecting with great interest the yards, the barns, the sheds, and the stock. Another sits at the warm fireside with the aged people, talking of the home affairs in-doors and out, — of wool, and grass, and poultry, and such other topics as properly appertain. And in this pleasantly placid way the chilly afternoon wears slowly by, the stream of talk swelling or shrinking with the change of moods and tenses there at the hearth. The pies and tarts and other like temptations that get baked in the huge kitchen oven before the night comes down to cover the chimneys, it would be idle to think of numbering.

Soon after ten o'clock, the next morning, as the tall clock in the corner makes musical proclamation, the several branches of the family tree are collected together in the living-room, prepared for meeting. They come from the chambers, from the kitchens, — where they have been indulging in a protracted strain of morning gossip, — from the stables, and the yards, and the barn. All are resolved to be talking at the same moment; now directly at one another, and now crosswise. An uncle fetches in an armful of hickory and maple, that there may be a rousing fire on the hearth when they return to dinner. Grandfather's hair shines like silver, brushed down so smoothly before and behind; and his white cravat and modest shirt-frill impart to him an extremely venerable appearance, which does not fail to challenge Grandmother's admiration, as she familiarly chats with children and grandchildren in her wonted corner.

There is a constant going to the glass at the further end of the room, and there is no end to the borrowing of pins, or to inquiries, one of the other, of how she "looked." A great deal of wondering, too, if there would be much of a turn-out at meeting. And much smoothing down of hair before, and brushing of coats and cloaks and capes. Till, presently, rattles around to the front door the grand family wagon, — a cross between a hay-cart and a chariotee, — followed by other smaller vehicles delegated to take up the family margin. Now the young people are in highest glee. They cannot find it in them to stand still, with such energy works the delight in their very feet and toes.

Along the roads, the trees are bared of leaves, save the storm-defying white oaks; while the fields stretch away on either side, bleak, snow-blotched, and desolate. A few wagons stand under the sheds about the meeting-house, whose owners are waiting and shivering just within the door. The Thanksgiving sermon is like itself alone; starting from an Old Testament text, of manifold divisions, full of a grateful spirit that takes at least half the year's credit to itself, and stuck all over with fervid allusions to the muscular souls that figure up and down the pages of Jewish scripture. It is a performance of *length* withal; but people endure that now far better than they do on the annual Fast Day. It smacks, too, of a home-flavor, and revives the dear old family memories, and is warmed with the wine of those associations which cluster about the domestic hearthstone. Just as much a part of the time as the annual dinner itself. Preliminary only to the "fat and sweet" that make festive indeed the family board. Linking together parents and children in still closer and more enduring bonds, — a kind of religious hyphen, that will let neither go.

After church comes Dinner. To this part of the celebration better justice can be done with the knife and fork than with the pen-point. For a while all stand or sit grouped around the open fire that is blazing in the dining-room, hungry and waiting. The talk is brief and brisk, touching no topic that promises to require much development. The long table is spread in the middle of the floor, extending almost from wall to wall. The younger girls, domestic by instinct, love to assist in bringing in the various dishes, making earnest fun of it on the way. One and another of the mothers present offer to help, but they are all begged to be patient for but a very little while longer, — only a little while.

In and out the door leading to the kitchen they troop, loading the tables and lightening themselves. The eyes around the hearth watch every movement eagerly. The tables are rapidly taking on an ornamental appearance. The boys *nudge* the girls, as some favorite dish is brought in and placed in full view, and their papillary glands are all awake for gratification. "Father" takes post at one end of the board, and deliberately runs his eyes up and down the same, to see if a single one out of so generous a flock may have been left out of the commissary's calculation. And finally, "Mother" walks in through the door from the kitchen, leisurely adjusting the cuffs of her sleeves, and then nods to Father that all is ready. He elevates his chin, as a sign of inquiry, to which she responds with a second nod. "Well," says he, "I believe dinner's *ready*. Won't you all please to be seated?"

How the intricate problem of seating them is solved, is a standing family mystery. Yet there they all are at last, snug and compact as herrings in a box, and with appetites beggaring description. The old folks are tenderly cared for, however, and occupy posts of honor. Parents and children, old and young, are sandwiched in about the board, imparting additional variety to the happy scene. The snow-white cloth, — the browned turkeys lying in state on huge platters in the middle of the table, — the flanking dishes of chickens, oysters, potatoes, squash, onions, celery, and other good things, — the handsome and well-kept old family service, tell the story of content and good cheer better than it can be set down upon paper. How delighted are the children with only the sight of the feast, exchanging smiles and telegraphing sly signals all around the table! How interestedly they watch the carving and disjointing of the fowls, as the white breast-meat falls away in such enticing slices from the sharp blade, and the anatomy of the subject becomes more and more palpable! And the preserves that have been brought forth from their dark hiding-places, — plum and pear and currant, — the jelly and sauce, too, how these tickle their youthful tastes even before contact, raising a livelier relish in their imaginations!

Hard by, on a sideboard conveniently placed, that is a perfect miracle and puzzle of drawers and doors and out-of-the-way apartments, are arrayed the bountiful rations of pastry and dessert. A large pudding and a smaller one, of custard and plum; together with manifold samples of the pies baked on the day previous, — mince, apple, squash, pumpkin, custard, and cranberry, and a very broad platter of tarts to match. The effect of all this side display is nowise lost upon the younger ones in the family party, nor indeed do the good housewives intend it shall pass unobserved of the elder participants of the festival. And there is tea as well, sending up its savory steams from the little side-stand, and waiting to be poured into the quaint little cups that are a genuine part of the homestead furnishing.

—— And thus this high feast of New England goes on. Knives and forks make a brisk clatter, and voices mingle and ring all over the room. All faces are lighted with the joy which all hearts sincerely feel. It is busy work, for a time, what with the eating and talking together; and the poultry carcasses show signs of giving out; while the puddings and pies melt away in turn; and, at last, the table exhibits but the wreck of the fat feast under which it so recently groaned. The children testify to their sense of surfeit by pushing back in their chairs and drawing difficult breaths. The older ones play with their knives or their tumblers, and essay short stories that require no great concentration of the faculties they have nearly put to sleep. Or the thrifty wives compare domestic receipts for this article and that, talking pints and pounds, sugar and juice, water and jars, till the snarl of household learning is hardly to be disentangled.

The evening brings its own pleasures again. Then the old-fashioned family games begin, — blind-man's-buff, puss-puss in the corner, snap-up around the chimney, forfeits, and their many ludistic congeners. The rooms all over the old house are lighted, and the echoes flock merrily up stairs and down. Grandfather has a smoky story in his corner for such as choose to gather round and listen; while Grandmother sits the centre of admiration for all the daughters and daughters-in-law assembled. And they keep it up till late bed-time. It is glee without limit or qualification. The hour is one with two figures, when the embers are buried on the hearth, and the lights are extinguished before the windows, and the crescent moon stoops low and virginal toward the western horizon.

But what a flood of happiness has swelled in every heart under the roof! Not a single head is laid upon its pillow, but is filled with dear thoughts of the endless and inexhaustible delights of Home. Not a heart but beats more strongly with genuine love for those simple and homely pleasures which mere wealth can neither give nor take away.

HARD WINTERS.

OLD people love to recount the trials *they* have passed through, eager to make it appear that the burden of this world's woes are fallen entirely upon themselves. The "last war" was a great deal harder to put up with than any boy's affair of these times; the famous "September Gale" has never been approached, for blowing capacity, by any tempest of more modern days; there never *was*, and never *will be*, such a depression of the public spirits as during the year of the "embargo;" and old-fashioned Winters have not been paralleled by the dismallest spells of cold weather that have latterly frozen men stiff and stark, at high noon, by the road side.

As far as downright hard winters go, it is more than likely they are in the right. Such snow-piles as they used to wallow and dig through, or ride upon when once safely encrusted, we do not chance to stumble into in these days, sure enough. Then they had sleighing four months on a stretch; whereas, if *we* can get even four weeks of it, the season through, we brag as lustily as if we had been exposed to trials as tough as any that encompassed the oldest inhabitants. Our mercury does sink pretty low, there's no denying it; but these "dreadful cold snaps" are never expected to endure for more than three days, when all the weather prophets assure us the cold has "got to its height," can go not one half degree further if it would, and must of necessity make way forthwith for a relaxing southerly rain.

We walk in "slosh" and mud, where our fathers went in whitest snow up to their knees. Frozen ice crunches under our tread, where the old settlers used to make the trodden snow-pavement squeal and squeak beneath their sturdy cowhide soles. Round-robin snow is enough to delight the children of this day; whereas their grandparents, at their age, would be out on the bleak country roads, helping the men "break out" with ox teams of a dozen and twenty to a string. In short, this is the millennial day of furnaces and double windows, of salted sidewalks and soft fur collars. In other times, they got warm out of doors, made friends with old Winter by defying him to do his biggest, and secured cheeks as ruddy as cranberries in October, that lasted them long after their hair turned silver.

To get at the good old wintry times once more, we must either go back into the years, or into the country. In these days, the latter is quite as convenient, if not a trifle more so. Away back at the homestead, they are all snugly snowed in during several months. They may get out, to be sure, at intervals far apart, when the travelling has become fair and the sunny days entice them, — as at Christmas, and New Year's, and, possibly, two or three times more before the Spring breaking-up; but, as a standing rule of faith, they are wont to consider themselves fixed, firm and fast, at the old domicil, from about Thanksgiving time till the freshets of the new season announce the coming of the frost from the ground. And the life at home there is thus made rich and deep, because it is not fragmentary, irregular, and without defined purpose. No family could be hived so warmly and comfortably in the snows of our northern latitudes for five long months, without finding out more of themselves and one another than they knew the autumn before.

What grown man of country nativity but

recalls the elegant sport he had, coasting down the long, winding New England hills with the girls, on the white moonlit evenings? — and does not wish, with a swift bound of his heart, that he could now find any side of the world as smooth a sliding-place as he found one side then, with Julia and Jane and Margaret on the sled in front of him? Then, the sparkle of the snow in the moonshine was not one half as full of gladness as the sparkle that danced in the eyes of the girls; nor were the reddest and richest tints that lay along the western horizon, in those wintry sunsets, a tithe as red and ruddy as those that made their young lips so ripe and fine. Then, the ring of the skater's steel up along the frozen creeks and coves made clearer music for the heart than any ring of voices or dollars since. And the sleigh-bell chime, sounding so deep and clear from that old strap that hung low beneath the white mare's belly, is incomparable, for sweetness and melody, with any of the vocal gymnastics or professional bell-ringing and tympanology of these modern days.

At school, the winter fun was not to be matched with any quality of sport had since. The dry, baking heat of the iron box-stove made the labor of erecting and defending snow-forts at noon-time a necessity as well as a delight; and the red hands, numbed with working in the frozen meal, burned like coals of fire as soon as the afternoon tasks within doors began again. And oh! the kicking and rubbing and plunging, from the chilblains! Torment was never devised for young rebels like this! Prisoners in Calcutta Holes, the world over, could experience no direr distress than did we children at school, from about half-past two o'clock in the afternoon until the hour arrived for us to be spelled round out of the little Walker dictionary. Many has been the winter's day, when I would joyfully have given all I possessed, or ever hoped to possess, for the freedom of the outside of the building, that, once there, I might take off shoes and stockings, and run wild like a colt in the snow! People talk of suspense as the acutest agony; it must be such have never had pesky chilblains in their childhood.

It is a long and difficult way home for the younger children, and so the older ones take hold together and draw little Sis on the sled, who hangs on as for dear life, sticking forward two red stockings as straight as a couple of candlesticks. But the raw journey has a delicious ending in the joy with which grandparents welcome us in the great living-room, and the kindness with which Mother urges us toward the fire, promising bread-and-butter in generous slices, the moment we are warm. And thenceforward till the thick darkness comes, it is the lad's work to go about home choring; getting in the wood for the night and the kindlings for the morning, tending the sheep in their sheds or the cows in their stalls, throwing down bedding and fodder, and taking an affectionate look by the way in upon the hens that have gone off early to roost. Sometimes he rebels in his little heart against the restraint this work imposes, especially if there happen to be a half-dozen other boys whom he would like to follow a half-mile further on the road, firing snow-balls as they go; but, generally, he performs his tasks well and truly, looking forward to the arrival of supper-time and the fairy evening scenes in the bright firelight afterward.

Yes, and it is the evening that remains crown and flower of all. The entertainments to be got by a child's imagination out of the pages of the "Arabian Nights," pale in their brilliancy before the delights that are extracted from these quiet and homely evening scenes, as they look to the boy who has progressed through weary experiences to riper manhood. The more rigorous the day's climate has been, the warmer and cosier the hearth at evening; the louder the wintry winds shriek at the windows and about the chimney-tops, the more bland and tropical seem the influences of the fire-heat at the hearthstone. The story is told; the lesson is conned for the morrow; or a neighbor drops in, and feels at once thoroughly welcome; or the old folks fall a-gossiping of the ancient days when people rode about in pillions, and make the younger ones fairly gape with strained attention. The golden words of Plato are not more golden to his handful of students and disciples, than are the hours of these winter evenings to all of us who have such on the roll to remember.

There were times, all along through these tough old winters, when the eaves would not drip for two and three weeks on the stretch, and on the south side of the house at that; when the horse-trough was tight frozen, and the farmers' beasts refused to turn up to it on their way along the road, comprehending the needlessness of the labor afar off; when the very poultry, for days together, were not to be seen huddled on the sunny side of the woodshed, preferring to stay close where the warm scents of the barn were a surer guarantee of comfort. Then the ice cracked with a sort of moan, pitched on a very low key, across all the ponds and coves and rivers. And the snow stuck like paint, or moss, to the sides of the forest trees against which it was plastered by the driving of the last storm. And the air was so still and cold, that the eyes turned to tears the moment they opened in its clear Arctic lake. And it were as easy to walk on pavements of brick and granite, as to set foot down upon the hard body of frozen snow that furnished the only floor for the world. And eggs split almost as soon as they were laid, — and cows refused to go out into the yard at all, — and the day was as still as the night, — and creation seemed to be waiting for a change in the weather before making another active movement. In these drear and silent nights of our northern winter, how thick stand the armies of the stars above, writing all over God's skyey dome in hieroglyphics that read with an eternal meaning!

There is one class of men, especially, that appears to appropriate all the out-door poetry of this rigorous and stern season; and they are the Wood-choppers. Sturdy Norse-folk indeed are they, emblazoned with frosty locks and beards, and toying like children with the winds that rush forth howling upon them from their lairs in the forest. Many a day have I envied the wintry lot of the wood-chopper. There seemed to be a nameless mystery in his occupation, that clothed him all over, in my eyes, with a garment of romance. He wandered off by faintly outlined cattle-paths, in the morning, into the woodland field of his labor, — axe under his arm, and dinner in the deep pocket of his green-baize jacket, — and was not heard from again until the coming of the red sunset. His long day, so uninterrupted and calm, so packed with thought, whole and entire in the solitude, and fragrant with the balm yielded by the cleft hearts of noble trees, was to my imagination like no other man's day, going through the whole line of the alphabet of names or professions.

He dealt out blows with his axe that rang like the strokes of fate along the aisles of the forest. The moan of the falling tree on the woodland slope was echoed in a low and dolorous key across the pond, and far into the dreary reaches on the other side. I have come upon him as he sat at his noon luncheon, too; under the lee of a rail-fence, or a fallen trunk, tossing crumbs and cheese-rinds around him for the partridges that have become familiar;

sunk clear down in the quiet lap of his own rude contemplations, and, now and then, taking the altitude of the solar disk, like any lonely mariner on his little deck in mid-ocean. I always liked to study the character and habits of these rugged, Saxon, hirsute, unflinching heroes of the wood; and deemed them the children of Winter, with thews and sinews toughened by the ceaseless assault of the winds, and nerves made steel by the frosts and snows they daily defied, and hearts all of knotty oak in the endless changes and chances of the weather.

This habit of hybernation, of literally going into "winter quarters," — like troops, or some animals, or the wiser sort of birds, — is just the one that gives to the season its attractive peculiarity; the difference between man and beast being this, that the former may so provide aliment for himself during this period that he need not actually consume his own increase, as bears are said by naturalists to "fall back on" their own fat. It is his period of *assimilation* rather, when he makes all that he has stored up really *his own* by an interior and genuine experience, acquired beneath his own roof and at the side of his own hearth.

Old men love dearly to sit about and tell —

so long as they can find believing listeners—of the hardships of *their* early winters, as of seasons out of the reach of parallels. A good deal of it, of course, comes of the lapse of years, whose wonderful mirage imparts its own exaggeration to every object and scene. In the village stores they meet on winter afternoons, and, after letting the snow melt from their heavy boots, rake over again the tough and charred knots that slumber in the embers of the past. There surely was never so cold a winter as that of eighteen hundred and—ever so far back; then, the post-rider had to travel on snow-shoes, and throw the mail-bags ahead of him as he went; then, the sleighing held good from before Thanksgiving till after the Governor's Fast; the roads were banked up and impassable for weeks together; the wild geese went south earlier than they were ever known to go before, and did not return till people had got almost tired of looking for them in the Spring; the squirrels were seen out upon the walls and fences but once, or twice at most, during the whole winter; and some sheep that got buried in the snow by accident, away over on a hill with a guttural Indian name, subsisted on one another's wool until they were discovered by their bleat and dug out into day again.

These stories are a sort of family heirloom; or, at best, they have root in the local soil, and help weave the sentiment of the neighborhood into a firmer social fabric. The cold snaps of December are a match for the sweltering heats of August; but people love better to rehearse the experiences of the former, just as they would rather dilate on vigorous contests they have borne a part in, than go over the scenes of a mere endurance, in which they were not permitted to strike a blow.

ONLY A LITTLE.

Not too much for me: a little will answer: —
  A roof that lets down its low, sheltering eaves,
An old apple-tree at the end of the garden,
  With a robin's nest hid in its chambers of
      leaves;
Some red honeysuckles in bloom on the ledges,
  A carpet of grass spread in front of the door,
A great rock lying down by the bars of the pas-
      ture,
  And chestnut-trees growing about in good store.

What larger want we than our snug little parlor?
  What cosier place than our porch in the rear?
We can sit in them through the sweet twilights
      of summer,
  And keep love alive through the whole of the
      year.
Could I love *her* the more in the grandest of
      mansions,
  Or feel her deep trust any more in great halls?
Would she seem just as dear in a hum of strange
      voices,
  As sitting here by me within our own walls?

These closely clipped lawns, and these fanciful vistas, —
These statues, and fountains, and gate-lodges, too, —
These swans on the ponds, in their afternoon barges, —
These stables, and kennels, and everything new : —
There is nothing about them that 's home-bred and simple,
As a footpath, a wicket, a rose by the wall;
I would not give up even one rustic treasure,
For the charm, or the cost, or the name of them all.

The meadow-brook makes me a right merry neighbor;
The quail plays his pipe through the hot afternoons;
The squirrels run over the old oak-tree branches;
And whippoorwills come in the summer-night moons.
Just over that hill are the sweet berry-pastures;
This other way stretch the deep woods where I roam;
The birds are awake in the gray of the morning;
And roses look into our windows at home.

It cost but a trifle: more love than hard money;
And so it will last us as long as love's store; —

'T is *the heart* that makes rich, or the whole life is pauper,
And happiness gets through the smallest sized door.
Not too much for me; no poor packhorse would I be,
To load up with riches for others to come;—
This world is compressed in the smallest of measures,
And the widest of realms is a dear little Home.

BOOK SECOND.

VICINAGE.

" *There is nothing like New England; and nothing in New England like its interior districts.*" — JUDD'S "MARGARET."

THE TOWN MEETING.

OUR only real democracy exists in the country towns. The rest is but limited and representative; while here it thrives in its original vigor and without restriction.

In the crowd of little towns that sprinkle the plains and crown the hill-tops of New England, independent sovereignties as they are, scenes as full of interest are annually presented — to the inhabitants and freeholders, certainly — as the Agora of Athens used to offer in that puissant and classic little city's palmy days. It is of just as much consequence who shall represent the town in the next legislature as, in Attic history, who was worthy to command the fleet, or lead the land forces against the invading Persians. The deliberation on local questions — as, how much money shall be appropriated for mending the highways, what tax shall be laid for enlarging the old school-house, and whether the township is determined to defend its sovereignty against the encroachments of a jealous neighbor,—provokes as much interest, and of as intense a character, too, as did any of those larger topics that swelled the soul of Demosthenes into phillipics which will be read by the latest generation that dwells on the planet.

At nine o'clock the bell rings,—the church bell. For the town meetings of the Homespun stamp are usually held in the meeting-house, where many an one secretly delights to take sly revenge on the sanctimonious necessities of his Sabbath-day conduct, and so goes about spitting and whittling pretty much as he will. The first work to which the assembled *demoi* address themselves, is that of choosing a Moderator; for a ship might as easily be worked without a compass or a helm, as a New England town-meeting try to get along without some controlling mind to tone down its waxing energy and enthusiasm. Generally, this imposing office is a gift to one of the deacons, if he is an elderly person, and the town be a small one; or, in case of contesting sectarian sentiments, it is laid with all sobriety upon one of the most staid and dignified out of the whole population. He assumes the office, not troubling himself to return thanks, however,—raps out order on the table with his tough knuckles, — and asks the assembly to listen with due devoutness to a prayer from the lips of the minister. This is a custom peculiarly of New England origin; and if it result in no positive good, it cannot be denied that it works no permanent harm. Perhaps the momentary hush of voices within better prepares the people to go seriously about the business of the day.

The Selectmen — an honored Board, that we can only pity the fierce Grecian democracies for having had to go without — range themselves near the Moderator; a clerk is chosen, who gets up and reads the "warning," — a copy of which may likewise be studied on the sign-post not far from the door; the business designated on the call is taken up in order, and forthwith proceeded with according to immemorial custom; and soon the general buzz of voices and shuffle of feet betoken the interest in which all are alike absorbed.

If it be Election Day, the people are directed by the Moderator, in a loud voice that is aimed at the singers' gallery, to prepare their votes for State Officers, members of Congress, Representatives to the Legislature, and Town Officers, to be deposited in the different ballot-boxes which he may designate, and to pass round — "if they please" — from the right to the left, — "to avoid confusion." This is the fun of the day. The contesting political parties have their challenging committees close to the polls, whose duty it is to dispute the right of one and another to vote, for reasons valid or trivial; these reasons being taken into the revolving thoughts of the row of Selectmen sitting close by, with countenances equally serious. One voter has n't lived in the town as long as he ought; another has been convicted of theft, or some other petty crime, and a certified copy of his conviction in court is all ready to be produced by the side challenging him. This one, now coming up with such an air of innocence, is directly going to be charged with the crime of not knowing how to read; and a copy of the Constitution being handed him, the work he makes over the hieroglyphics of its *letters* can be paralleled by nothing better than the ignorance of scores around of anything akin to its *meaning*. The energy with which this challenging business is pushed, and the tough tenacity with which the doubt or denial of another's capability as a voter is made good, are excellent illustrations of those qualities of character that make the New England man exactly what he is, and nothing different, as his friends farther to the South would have him.

When the voting on Representatives grows sluggish, the Moderator straightens his legs and asks them, in that same Olympian tone, if they "are all voted;" soon after which, the counting by the Selectmen begins, others having meanwhile stood by and kept tally on their own account. Now it becomes exciting indeed. It may be the vote is very close; in that case, the outside counters and tally-men are as much in the dark as the rest, since they may have been deceived in their expectations from a few men's ballots, not knowing which side offered them the latest drink at the tavern.

Oftentimes it is announced from the Chair, that "there has been no choice, and you will therefore please prepare your votes again." This moderatorial edict is echoed up in the bell-tower, a few pulls at the clapper proclaiming to all stragglers, and to those who would like to go home after voting once, that it is necessary to go over it all again. And then begins the tug of war. The whippers-in of each party fall upon their victims with the rapacity of harpies. One never before witnessed, and never will again, such personal partiality of the high for the low, and the clean for the unclean; nor heard such protestations of undying friendship and devotion. It will take but *one* more vote, — or two, or three, to carry this thing clear over to our side! — and the zeal flames up in astonishing disproportion to the chances.

Perhaps, even the next time, no election is effected; nor the next, nor the next. Then the Statute makes provision for the case, and another election is ordered for another day. But the *general* tickets are not taken from the boxes and counted and proclaimed, until the hour limited by the law has passed; before which time, a pretty strict tally having been kept through the day by party lieutenants, it is generally known how the balloting stands, and a small knot only is therefore collected about the polls. When, however, the general result *is* declared, some enthusiastic partisan always stands ready to give the bell-rope a vigorous twitch or two in honor of his own side, and it is understood all through the town that election is finally over. A new notch has been nicked in the town's history.

A great deal of interest is let down upon this occasion through the side-lights; that is to say, the oyster-stands near the horse-sheds and about the "Green," as well as the sly drinking scenes over at the tavern, or in the little back-room of the grocery store, furnish many a needed illustration for the work more legitimately performed in the meeting-house. To suppose that a New England election could be successfully conducted without the help of stewed oysters, eaten out of blue-rimmed bowls with pewter spoons, is to betray the ignorance of the person who ventures the conjecture. Or to believe that a due head of partisan steam could be kept up without regular and repeated levies on the casks of Boston rum, that are tucked away in the dark recesses of the back-store over the way, is evidence of a lack of familiarity with these matters, not to be pardoned in any native commentator. Then there is much character to be studied in the talk that goes on among the knots sprinkled about the doors, across the road, out near the horse-sheds, and over the Green. The Congressional Debates reported for years in the "Globe," will bear but a slender comparison with these for originality of views, cogency of reasoning, or close personal application. Every son of his mother in New England is a born talker, save only the tongue-tied ones; and he does no talking so thoroughly as this to which he "calculates" to devote himself on town-meeting day.

They hold a second convention of the sovereigns, in another season of the year; when the strictly local interests are debated and disposed of as they ought to be. At this they choose their selectmen, justices of the peace, tithing-men, and — greatest of all — fill the ancient and honorable office of "hog-reeve." In many localities this last popular gift is as highly esteemed, and bestowed with quite as much seriousness, as those other ones which bring the recipients a little more prominently before the eyes of the world. In others, however, it has mysteriously parted with its ancient dignity, and is not much better than a pasquinade, to fling at the head of some one who happens either to be odious or the town butt. An instance of sharp retaliation for the unexpected bestowal of this honor just now occurs to me. A certain Judge, — a man of large attainments and sharp-edged sarcasm, — who found himself one day elevated to this position by a secret conspiracy among those whom he had not altogether pleased hitherto, seeing the delight with which his election was greeted, stepped up on one of the benches next him, and blandly asked if those who had been good enough to vote for him would gratify him so much as to rise in their places. Nothing daunted, the conspirators got up in a defiant body, meeting his open look with their ill-suppressed jeers. "Ah! that will do!" returned the Judge; "I thank you. I only wanted to see *about how many hogs I had got to have the care of!*" Scrupulous care was had, after that year, in offering to others an honor which had once disgraced none but those who bestowed it.

—— The natural aptitude for affairs that so marks the character of the men of New England, is discoverable here in their little town-meetings. There is many a young fellow, just through his college studies, who would gladly exchange all his acquired readiness in translating the Greek and Latin poets for the practical, up-and-down knowledge of a respectable selectman, or town assessor. As for the science of debate, it would be hard to find bodies of men anywhere who could utter as much in so few and pointed words. If they do debate a matter, it is not for the sake of displaying their reading or their rhetoric; but they go straight to the core of it, and make it appear very shortly whether a new proposition, or plan, is likely to be "worth the while" or not. That is the mighty touchstone of all their views. The same thrift that puts the individual on the road to independence, is made to pave the town's highway to power.

—— And these are the men who hold in their hard and honest hands the safety of our country, — of our all. Verily, the town-meeting is the nursery of the national life. In this little and remote assembly are fashioned the principles of the men that make us just what we are before the world.

THE COUNTRY STORE.

FOR lack of theatre, music hall, fantoccini, or riding in the Park, the people of the interior districts are compelled to fall back on something else in the line of amusement, than which no entertainment could well be held in higher esteem. It is the Country Store. This modest "institution" is as distinct, too, and well defined in the social landscape as the spire of Trinity, or the gray shaft on Bunker Hill.

The whole population of the neighborhood resort to it with regularity; — all the loungers, all the idlers, all who have done up their weary day's work, all the town gads and gossips in trousers, as well as all those who go for molasses in jugs, for nails, tobacco, and raisins, — loiter, and talk, and listen in this most convenient place of public reception. And if store and Post-office chance to be combined, the flocking of the sovereigns, with wives and offspring, fairly puts one out in any attempt at description. Besides the sugar, nails, tea, codfish, soap, and brooms, there lie all the letters that are addressed personally to the men and women of the town.

—— Truly, an item to be thought of. The sum total of all their correspondence with the strayed-away cousins, nieces, nephews, and children. Therefore at this little hive the swarming town collects. Therefore do they come hither, evening after evening, picking up waifs of news and watching like paid detectives the postmaster's distribution of the letters. Therefore do they hustle and bustle around that functionary's person when the mail-bag is fetched in from the coach, and proffer assistance in assorting the miscellaneous newspapers which he empties over the counter. Offering advice, when it is needed and when it is n't. Submitting comments — original and assorted — on all classes of topics, with such sly foot-notes as one may not at first understand.

Then a country store is a strangely quiet place, of an afternoon, whether in summer or winter. Save when, perhaps, some little girl patters in to exchange a skein of thread, the flies and the rural merchant have it entirely to themselves. If the place is in charge of a spruce young clerk, in lieu of the master, he employs himself with brush and oils at the little cracked mirror behind the high desk, and lets the flies sun themselves in sleepy knots over the floor.

It is not less a realm of doziness, either, in planting-time, and through the sweaty spell of haying. In the former season, the men are about the gardens and off over their farms, and a fox might take a leisurely trot through the town street without attracting the eye of master or hound. Perhaps an enterprising pedler, atop of a bright red wagon, trundles up to the door-step, and, from his canopied box, "passes the time of day" with the prompt clerk, asks for latest news, and offers essences at the *very* lowest "figger." Or a stray cow comes tearing off the succulent grass like silk near the door, perhaps with a bell strapped about her neck, and putting the town more completely to sleep with its somnolent melodies.

This is the store in the country town, or the village. It sometimes stands, however, away by itself at the crossing of two roads, with the proprietor's dwelling in close propinquity; its entire front protected from burglars by the ancient swing-shutter, and barricaded with boxes and buckets, half filled with beans and dried apples and oats, that are tilted on the broad shelf just under the window; — I do not believe a lonelier spot can be found in the whole range of puritan New England; a mill-pond in a faded December afternoon is a place of resort, by comparison, — a hemlock thicket at sunset is noisy in contrast with its sepulchral desolateness.

But when farming does not drive, and leisure is to be had in solid junks by all who want it, the store is not altogether so bare of interest to the casual observer. Huddled as the talking population love to be found, their portraits, or full-lengths, may then be readily taken. The men and the boys, perched on barrels or the counters, either swing their feet and gossip, or swing their feet and spit. If it is winter, they cuddle up to the dull box-stove, and polish the long pipe with their hard palms as coolly as if they were salamanders. They are stowed in unseen corners, too, — the young fellows in particular, — where they work over colorless, but sometimes rank, jokes in half whispers, and snicker in nasal unison over their odd confidences about the girls. The small boys drink in what falls, grinning bashfully when the larger ones laugh; they are taking their early lessons faithfully and well.

Of winter evenings, the stove, crammed with seasoned sticks, roars like any menagerie lion.

No January winds without can drown its growling sound. The loungers are gathered in a great open circle, each with a hand erected for a screen. There it is the affairs of the nation are sifted; there each town sovereign closes and grapples with his dissenting neighbor, and finds his own personal niche among those occupied by the local worthies. The minister's last sermon comes up for analysis at this rustic round-table; when the astonishing fact is revealed, that they are all not less profound theologians than marvellous masters of state craft and civil polity.

Or, on topics of gallantry, of reputation, of property, of talents, — this is the Country Club to begin at the beginning, and not leave off till the end. I have many a time sat and wondered, looking at them thus engaged, what possible escape-valve would serve their turn, if this free-and-easy privilege at the store should chance to be cut off! If they talk only unqualified scandal *now*, they might be guilty of the sin of provoking it *then;* — and which, I beg to know, on your conscience and honor, would be worse? If *some* of us may not serve the turn of harmless local historians, or annalists, then we must, perforce, go at it as heroes, and become naughty men.

—— One may as well style the country store the Forum for the town in which it stands. Neither the Forum at old Rome, nor the Agora at Athens, showed greater in their own way and day. It is a really homespun institution, — everything we have is an "institution," in this country, — and wears like the sterling fabric's own self. Here are held the local debates, nightly, as in Parliament, through the cold weather. Here issues are joined, and the tallow candles flare applause or sputter disapprobation.

—— Or, you may say it is the place of the town assizes. In some country settlements, there are men who are bloody Jeffreys at heart, delighting to bully the rest with their decisions, and permitting neither appeal nor extenuation. In others, you will find honest Matthew Hales enough to keep sweet the whole body of public sentiment by their fair, open, and well-balanced judgments. For judgments are to be made up, — *must* be made up; that being the "chief end of man," in these little social bailiwicks.

—— To the store flock the farmers, in earnest with their spring work, after seeds and manures and agricultural implements. Boys run thither on errands for their mothers, their sisters, and themselves. Thrifty housewives drive up before the door at an early forenoon hour, in the summer time, and go in to make barter of eggs, and cheese, and stocking-yarn for cotton cloth, or calico, or new shoes with a proper "power" of squeak in them. The girls flock, with red blushes burning in their cheeks, to see if anything lies over for them in the mail, or to exchange a few words with the sleek-haired clerk, or to finger, for the twentieth time, the limited stock of berages, prints, and mousselin de laines which he ever stands ready to spread about the counter.

You will see a whole caravan of old family cobs about the premises, some with bob-tails and some with switch, holding down their heads and drowsing away the hours as if they had cropped poppy-heads instead of green clover, for their summer morning repast. And elderly females are visible, too, climbing friskily into and out of their open wagons, the day's successful barter giving them the nerve required to keep them from falling.

As politicians, the men who gather statedly at the country store strain the limits of common comprehension. On city rostrums, it is thought the political notorieties sometimes give a start to the public pulse; but at the store, the work is personal, and striking, and thorough, beyond example. They make it their grand point here to *corner* a man; after which operation, it is thought he is not worth putting forth much strength upon. It is held to be the coronal feature of argumentative skill and power, to get an opponent "where he can't get away." And so it is, according to Socrates himself, who had an awfully teazing way of putting questions; — or agreeably to Father Aristotle, who led by the nose the rest of the dialecticians of his day, and impressed his system on all the schools of Europe after him. To "argue the point" is esteemed one of the divine Rights of Man; and no government or authority shall dare take it out of their hands.

Yet no *two* persons are permitted the luxury of having it all to themselves; the rest claim their privilege of breaking down the ropes of the ring, and taking a hand as well. Political newspapers are published chiefly for these very friends of ours, who devour them as eagerly as rich men once used to consume widows' houses. For them the bulky "Congressional Debates" are printed (on execrable contract paper) by authority of Congress; and to their columns they repair for ammunition with the regularity of artillerists in action to caissons and portable magazines. No good deacon, zealous beyond discretion, ever hurled texts at the head of a doubter with such overwhelming effect, as do these native balearists rain down dates, names, and quotations on the battered skulls of political contestants. Theirs the task of Cerberus and Rhadamanthus both; they form the Caucus, — the Congress, — the real Democracy. Wars and rumors of wars; elections and estimated results; reputations, both public and private; cases in court, — the doctrinal soundness of the minister, — the state of the crops and the weather; — none think themselves their equals in the discussion and disposal of these topics all.

—— It is excellent for an open and sunny heart, in the autumn season, to let the eyes run round among the crook-necks, and yellow mastodons of pumpkins, and barrels of clean, white beans, and thin-skinned potatoes, that garnish and stuff out the apartment, from ceiling to cellar-door. The store has then been transformed into the town museum of agriculture. Here the good farmers hold their in-door local shows; here quietly rehearse the labors of the season just ending, and estimate personal gains in oats, corn, and potatoes. They make calculations on the number of cows they will winter, and compute (in money) the amount of fleece wool the "wimmen folks" will get carded and rolled for the cold-weather season of spinning. Their talk is of crops, of fruit, horses, sheep, and cattle;—of girth, and draught, and year-olds, and fattening by stall-feeding.

If you ever drive through one of these back towns in pleasant weather, it will pay you well to feed your beast a half-peck of oats (last year's are best, the farmers say,) in the feeding-trough under the shed, and lounge into the store yourself for the pure recreation of seeing and being seen. The store-keeper will not be behind with substantial civilities; you shall make no complaint for lack of attention from the gathering bystanders until your horse has eaten his last oat and set up a neighing for more; and the inevitable codfish and string of onions hanging on the outside wall will haunt you with dreams of traffic and commercial adventure, till you even set foot on Long Wharf again and welcome the coasters from the Banks and Old Weathersfield.

THE COUNTRY TAVERN.

IT was a sort of half-way house between home and the open world. You might style it Home on the Road. It was the limit where the shyer and tenderer domestic feelings began to let go their hold, and give place to the bold and bustling influences of the world. The hotel of the city has little in common with the tavern of gone-by days, and can scarcely claim kinship. That was a peculiar social construction, shaped and furnished exactly to the purposes it was to serve. We find nothing like it in these times, not even in the country itself.

On the subject of inns, Dr. Johnson's dictum may be worth quoting again: — "No, sir," said he, "there is nothing which has yet been contrived by man, by which so much happiness is produced as by a good tavern or inn." And he was fond of repeating Shenstone's well-known lines in support of his sentiment: —

> "Whoe'er has travelled life's dull round,
> Where'er his stages may have been,
> May sigh to think he still has found
> The warmest welcome at an inn."

The romances of Sir Walter are full of inns of every name and character. There is inn talk of the most attractive sort in "Don Quixote" and "Gil Blas." Sterne and Smollett and Fielding carry us off by the arm to the nearest tavern, where good cheer abounds, and care is soon dissipated, and the hard walls of real life become the merest boundaries of air.

Shakspeare, too, was a confirmed tavern haunter, and knows not how to keep it a secret in his comedies. Multitudes of his finest fancies flew up to the clear sky of his mind while sitting in his favorite "Boar's Head" at Eastcheap. Ben Jonson — "rare Ben" — was altogether at home in the tavern's inspiring purlieus; and ruled the roast there in the midst of his learned and witty compeers. Dryden sat at "Will's," dispensing oracles and judgments to listening circles for all London. But jolly Sir John, — that hero without courage, that never-full butt of old-fashion sack, — he remains chief and hugest of all tavern-haunters of any abiding repute. His great creator conceived him in the heart of the place where the best of his corpulent life was spent.

Everybody who reads knows his habit of taking his ease in his own inn.

The wits of Charles the Second's time, and of Anne's, were wont to make of the tavern their council chamber; and at length it became a forcing-house for all the sayings, fine and coarse, that delighted the town or provoked to reading. Who loved the old haunts better than Dick Steele, — that pattern of unthrift and preacher of true gallantry? Who could conceive, in their little back-rooms, a nobler Cato, or profounder judgments on the genius of Milton, or an honester country 'squire than Sir Roger de Coverly, than Addison, with his black bottle at his elbow? And there was poor Burns, — he frequented the taverns when he would better have been at the tail of his plough, turning up mice-nests and mountain daisies; and yet the tavern more or less fed his genius, as it lagged and loitered along the rough road he was destined to travel.

Going backwards again: one takes it to heart like a pleasant experience of his own, to read what old Izaak Walton, father of all good and quiet anglers, said and did, when himself and Venator came, early in the morning, to the little inn where the room was stuck about with ballads on the wall, and the white sheets of the hostess had such a sweet smell of lavender: — "I 'll now lead you to an honest alehouse, where we shall find a cleanly room, lavender in the windows, and twenty ballads stuck about the wall."

This ideal inn, which Father Walton describes with such enticing simplicity, is the very one that, of all others, has taken captive our fancy. In lieu of scents of sour sack and spoiling punch, we seem to smell the sweet savors of primrose and dill, and the delicate boquet of the bottle of elderberry wine which the hostess takes down so choicely from the cupboard.

—— An old tavern used to be, in the days I am calling up again with such fondness, the synonym of comfort and repose and plenty. We have few or none of these ancient affairs left now. They and the stage-coach were twinned in the inventor's brain; and when one fell into disuse, it was natural for the other to pass out of mind also. To keep tavern without the grand feeder of a stage line would have been making bricks without straw.

The railways have, with a merciless straight-line energy, cut and slashed up the pleasant old solitary turnpikes and quiet by-roads where the stage-coach once rattled its wheels and smacked its whip, — and the life-blood of ancient tavern-keeping has thus been drained off into a swifter channel; so that "entertainment for man and beast" put away its dusty but honest toggery, and followed the style and whim of the railway. Hence, if you look for "entertainment," — which socially implies what is domestic and cheerful for the tired traveller, you will now find nothing more than "refreshments," — which mean a sanded floor, wire-dish covers in blue, swarms of flies, and a coming train. Ah! but these times are not those times! The sorriest of it all is, too, that none of us will live to know the broad and hearty reality of the by-gone days again!

Still, it is due to posterity that the memory of the Old Tavern, and of the many kind offices it has so cheerfully performed for humanity, be kept green. Let us live it all over again, though it be but in the reproduction of a youthful dream.

—— In the first place, and to begin at the beginning, it was a wonderful mart for coaches. They stood under almost every shed that made a convenient lean-to in the spacious yard, and in nearly every stage of existence, — from the freshly varnished one, just come in, to the pot-bellied old veteran that had patiently carried well-nigh a whole generation over the hills. On some the dust was piled thickly; stable-boys were busy washing up the wheels of others; here and there was a decrepit customer, unquestionably crippled by an uncalculating whip with a cruel overload; but the prevailing expression of the yard was that of coaches. Had the place been cleaned of them at a single vigorous sweep, it would have looked as empty as a library with the books gone from the shelves.

In the centre of this tavern court-yard, a pump, with a jolly squeak that seemed to start up business all about the place. Horses were led out to the great trough under its nose, and sometimes slipped away from the boys who led them, snorting and tearing back to the stable again. A long and broad "stoop" behind the low-roofed house, whereon were set pails, pans, baskets, and other housekeeping utensils, — a very miscellaneous assortment. Beds crammed out through the upper back windows, for a brief morning airing. Doves wheeling and tumbling about, or setting up their monotonous domestic cries close under the barn eaves.

There used to be a wide and spacious hall reaching from the front entrance of the house, and a broad and inviting porch, the picture of hospitality, with an ample seat on either side, projected to correspond. It was all smooth and faultlessly clean about the door, the short grass making a green margin for a sufficient drive for vehicles of all sorts, and many at a time, to come up composedly before the windows. Lights were flashing, and cheery wood-fires blazing in the great square rooms when the laden coach rattled up to the door, just at night in late autumn; and never was sincerer welcome extended to weary souls away from their own home-hearth, than came playing and dancing forth from those flames into their eager eyes. The pursy landlord — best evidence of his own tavern-fare — bustled in and out of the rooms, explaining to one where he could be accommodated with "travellers' rest," and showing another into the wash-room, — now stirring up the fire with a fresh inspiration of industry, and now suddenly retreating to answer a call in the low-studded bar-room. He made himself genial to all; put general questions, and made general answers to all particular ones; and gave over no personal effort until he saw for himself that every man, woman, and child had fallen naturally into place in his own family circle, and satisfied his honest judgment that they were thoroughly comfortable and happy.

He? — why, bless your heart! he made it a point in his education as an accomplished publican, to qualify himself to "talk politics" — though not to venture upon discussion — with every judge, lawyer, and public character whom the coach — which to him stood for the world — might please to bring to his door. He would have felt illy adapted to his station, had he come short in so important a particular. Nowadays, the very boys talk politics, with unabashed vociferousness; and even the women, too; and the wise man is he who shuts tight his lips and stays, like a hermit or a turtle, with his own wisdom at home. All the ministers, the country round, he knew by creed and name; and he would dispense as full and fair a judgment on both, in a few shrewdly wise phrases, as they could themselves have passed on their own doctrines and in their own pulpits. He was the *genius loci;* and unless his familiar and effulgent countenance was seen of the traveller as he drove up to share his welcome entertainment, he seemed to have missed of the pith of his visit altogether. For food and lodging were not quite all the stranger expected to find there; he looked for a share of the landlord's cheery greeting and cordial conversation.

Between the people of the neighborhood and their wonted social recreations he served as a sort of connecting link, or substantial hyphen; if anything was going on, or was likely to go on, our jolly host could whisper you all there was to it, because it had been invariably concerted at tavern headquarters. More business — in the line of pleasure — was here set on foot than anywhere else in the town or the country round about. The landlord must needs be consulted about the next ball, or the select cotillon party, or the harvest supper of a circle of old-friend farmers, or on matters of that sort. Was there a squirrel hunt in the autumn? Never until the arrangements for picking clean their little bones at the long table in his dining-room had all been gone over with so much care, and the whole cost and outlay duly estimated at his hands.

If a drover stopped over night with him, he could answer every one of his inquiries for local news while he was twirling the toddy-stick in his customer's punch at the bar. Would a family party, on an excursion of pleasure across the country, "put up" with him till next morning? — he was at the door as quick as they were at the step themselves, and made it hard for them to believe they had wandered very far from their own threshold, after all. The man, in fact, was like his inn, — broad, welcoming, sunny, domestic, full of light and life, and withal as plain as he was sincere. These later times seem to demand no such characters in their hasty service, and therefore none such are to be found.

The stage-coach driver was a feature of the Old Tavern, as distinct as the landlord's self. Muffled, in winter, in his huge gray woollen tie, and nested in warm robes that defiantly flung off the icy arrows of the season, he was the passing envy of half the rosy girls and all the little boys the country round. What a reverberating ti-ra-tir-a-la! he shook out from the nozzle of that well-worn horn of his, as he crept over the summit of the hill from which he could see the roofs and smokes of the Tavern! Countless were the errands entrusted to his elastic memory, and his perennial spring of good-nature made their prompt discharge worth double what they were taxed for in his daily reckonings. He was, perforce, in the confidence of half the girls along the road; and they would have felt sadly slighted if he had failed, even for a single time, in the dexterous acknowledgment of their stolen smiles and glances. He could tell you, if he so chose, and if you were lucky enough to ride on the box with him, who was likely to "catch" this one, and who not long ago "got the mitten" from that. A very fund, nay, a strong-box of dear little secrets was he, and the key was kept hid where none but the owners of their property could find it for themselves.

At the Tavern were consummated cattle swaps and horse trades uncounted. It served for their Exchange; and never did a dicker or a jockey occur, but the profit and the loss were each congratulated and consoled with sundry social drinks at the bar. At all hours of the day, and through all seasons of the year, a fly, a sulky, or a skeleton gig could be seen somewhere about the yard, the property in horse-flesh changing hands so rapidly that one could with difficulty trace it along to its last holder. In fact, the capacious stables were pied and mottled inwardly with all varieties of steeds, from the showy and shiny bay to the ewe-necked and cat-hammed drudge of the shiftless jockey; and their study would have held the eye of the naturalist not less than of the fancier.

The upper hall, of winter evenings, frequently blazed with multitudinous tallow lights, and resounded to the inspiring strains of violin and clarionet. There the good folks enjoyed hearty times indeed; no mincing and tossing while the airs of Strauss were played so divinely, — no loud and rude estimates, such as one is compelled to hear now, of the value of the very clothes one had on, or of a partner's necklace, already blooming and bouncing enough in modest muslin, — but right-down enjoyment all round on the spot, as if that was the very thing they came for. And they never went home without having it. Nor were the other occasions of the year at all cast into the shadow by these sundry ball-and-party "good times"; the suppers and private feasts enjoyed under that sheltering roof were matters to stick by the memory of a man long after their flavors were lost to his palate. Thus did the dull days shut in as much pleasure there as the sunny ones; it was all sunshine at the Old Tavern, and the prime expression of the place was one of comfort and warmth and careful attention.

Of summer evenings, through the lingering twilight, a row of respectable idlers — the professional loungers of the town — used to be drawn up on the low, long benches set against the house, whose heaviest responsibilities as a body were to discuss the affairs of town and nation, and pass judgment on such vehicles, with their contents, as chanced at that dreamy hour to come up. This bench was a sort of idlers' paradise; he who sat on it must certainly have had his lids touched by the wing of somnolency, for thereafter he seemed to have no care, and scarcely to entertain a serious thought. It was like drifting in one's skiff off into the region of sunset. A drowsy knot they were, enjoying the noiseless twilight, the shelter of the great elms, the quiet bustle going on in-doors, and the sleepy influences of their own low hum of talk.

—— But the Old Tavern, alas! is no more. You may travel off among the hills and up and down the ancient pikes of New England in quest of it, but you don't find it there now. The structure may still be standing where it did, but it is a comparative solitude now; no life about the yard, — no swarming in and out the doors, — no cheerful faces close to the windows, — nor fires on the hearths, — nor lights and music in the halls. Travellers go not now by that way; but skim the ground a dozen miles to the east or west of it, little thinking of the substantial pleasure their fathers and mothers enjoyed in that now neglected place, when to travel was to trundle over the roads at the rate of forty miles a day, instead of the hour, and stop at all the excellent taverns that once formed a chain of posts from southern New England to the farthest lines of the Canadas in the wilderness.

THE COUNTRY MUSTER.

ARMA, virumque cano, — or, at least, a whole Regiment and its Colonel.

Rub-a-dub! rub-a-dub! — The memory is quickened with scouting thoughts of Cæsar, of Marlborough, and of Israel Putnam. One tries in a moment to think of all the great sieges in history, from that of old Troy down to the later one of Vicksburg; of battles, and skirmishes, and victories, and retreats; of beleaguered Antwerps, and Netherland Revolts, and Peninsular Wars; of grimy cannoniers, and clashing sabres, and rattling spurs. And still it can be heard a full half-mile off, far away over the green-sward plain, — Rub-a-dub! rub-a-dub! rub-a-dub!

The little fellows, on the way to training in company with their fathers, can scarcely touch their heels to the ground. Every breath of wind that wafts to their ears a faint roll of the martial music, stirs their impatience to put behind them all the rods that lie between their feet and the camp-ground. As they come still nearer, and see the rows of dingy booths that serve for tricky margins to the martial show, with fiddles squealing, and dancing going forward, — oysters, hot coffee, gingerbread, and pies cried in their ears, — pedlers hawking their cheap wares from the tops of wagons, men and boys straggling about among the carts, some singing drunken songs that overrun with drowsy riot, some mimicking the tones of the noisy auctioneers, the women mingled in with the men all along in front of the military lines, — they feel, at length, as if the summit of their year's hopes had been reached, and every heart-beat responds to the tattoo of the inspiring drumstick at the head of the regiment.

The great "*campus martius*" presents the usual motley of so fantastic a festival. There is nothing in all history before it, from the hustling times of the Crusades to the scientific defeat of Napoleon at Waterloo. Frederick of Prussia never plumed himself more on his famous grenadiers than does the regimental Colonel on the all-sizes under his command, — "*Decus et tutamen in armis.*" There he is in the saddle now! How proudly that best piece of horse-flesh in the county takes his martial paces across the turf he spurns! How gayly glitter the epaulettes of his rider — how gracefully waves his plume — how noisily jingle his regimental trappings! He must assuredly feel as if the neck of his steed was "clothed with thunder." Achilles did not rush more eagerly into the Trojan meleé to avenge his well-beloved Patroclus, than does our gallant Colonel dash up to his noble column, that he may prance his horse showily down the lines as far as to his valiant ensigns. — O War! War! little knowest thou of the bloodless farces that have been annually performed in old pastures and quiet back-lots in thy name! We need a Cervantes, to show up as it should be done the *pleasanter side* of thee!

—— The wagons from all the quiet farm-houses for miles around are collecting as fast as they can, and the horses taken out and baited with the bundles of hay from behind the seat; all about the grounds is an encampment of farmers' turn-outs, the owners having sprinkled themselves over the martial plain. The neighing of old mares — *hinnitus equarum*, as Virgil might say, — makes one think of the vast preparations of old time for expeditions against the Infidels, when all the paraphernalia of war were mixed up in distracting confusion, — booths and heroes and armor and smiths. All comers are "tidied up" in their best suits, and not a boy — unless of the fighting class who go to such places — but wears as smooth and clean a collar as his good mother at home could fold and pin about his tawny neck. Ah! but this is peculiarly the boys' own day; this is the great harvest time for huge sheets of gingerbread, small beer, and Sicily oranges. If they have been hoarding up the proceeds of woodchuck skins, and the margins accruing from sharp-sighted traffic in small miscellanies, for months past, it was but to this most worthy end; they kept their imaginations at white heat by dwelling on the sweetened luxuries of the coming Muster.

The regiment — as any military man will tell you — is broken into companies; you can see the several captains, short and tall, standing forth all the way down the line, fixed and rigid under the load of their holiday responsibilities. Somewhere among them stand our Scotts and Taylors that are to be, and the whole corps of our Worths and Wools and McClellans. They know it, and the county round about knows it; and peace is therefore secure. But the pied uniforms impart a mosaic appearance to the field, that could not otherwise be so skilfully produced by any device of mortal man. Some of the companies are clad in true-blue from top to toe, buttoned up all tight and right; while their neighbors wear black swallow-tails over ample seats of white, whose natural extensions flap their folds in the wind all the way down their legs. Artillery-men carry on their heads great, heavy, bell-shaped hats of leather, surmounted with a yellow stub of a pompion; and over each man's two shoulders creep a pair of yellow woollen caterpillars, possibly denoting that "*in hoc signo*" they are bound to fire as good guns, and as loud, as the best of them. Every captain wears a monster chapeau, that unfortunately half swamps the eyes of the little fellows, and diminishes to that extent their native expression; while a red sash either encircles the waist of the slim ones, or makes an indented equatorial line around the abdomen of the corpulent. When the proper field officer, stiffening his legs in the stirrups, orders them to "march," such a lifting of long legs and such a stretching of short ones, for some three or four paces forward, is not to be seen and enjoyed among the grenadiers of old Europe, or the *chasseurs* of modern Africa either. Then they face about again, and march back to their lines with all the satisfaction of commanders just returned from victorious war. The captains are the "representative men" of their companies; "*ex uno disce omnes.*"

In all these rural regiments there are two elements, — the volunteers and the militia. The latter used to be honored with the patriotic title of "mi-*lish.*" It was the glory and boast of these "regulars" that they trained but twice a year, paid their fines when they preferred to do that, and uniformed themselves after rules and patterns the most discordant and diverse. Some with light trousers, and some with dark; now and then one in his shirt sleeves — his family coat of arms; and, here and there, one in a very wide-brim straw hat. All styles of toggery, — hats, caps, and straws; jackets, swallow-tails, and frocks; six-footers and lilliputians; men with the lean and hungry look of Cassius, and men with the proportions of our ancient friend Falstaff; hirsute and shaven; shouldering rusty fowling-pieces and little stumpy rifles; brandishing bayonets and drilling with hickory-sticks; — all a medley of men, arms, and clothing, that would have divided public admiration with the ill-assorted heroes of Coventry.

—— Such the field. A loosely linked chain

of versi-colored parts, stretched like a huge serpent along the ground. At the head, a corps of drummers and fifers, commanded by a musically-given major, who cuts off their tunes with a professional twinkle of his sword-blade. When the drums begin their roll, after the routine of regimental drill is over, the vast encampment wakes up from centre to circumference. All the boys make a rush for the music, and all the sentries straddle across the enclosure at the top speed of a walk, to head them off or die in the attempt. The girls and the mothers testify their martial spirit by a new flash of the eye and flush of the cheek, and involuntarily keep time with the beat of the drum-sticks. The staid family beasts standing round prick up their ears, many of them recognizing the very same music that was drummed out in that very same place, years ago, in their coltish youthfulness. The din around the refreshment booths is for a few moments hushed, and the laughter of the sons of Ham temporarily gives way to the only enjoyment which can claim successful competition.

Now they form in sections, some of the ranks so crooked that no military genius could ever hope to make them stand still. The

Colonel is at the head of the column, with sword poised over his shoulder; and his staff take subordinate positions, according to the rigid forms of military law. "Forward—*march!*" How the order rings far down over the heads of the phalanx in arms! It is caught up by all the big captains and the little captains, and whole lines of legs are simultaneously stretched to measure a two-foot pace, according to the local manual. The fifes set up their scream. The snare drums roll long waves of music down the column. The bass drums come thumping in with their swelling musical emphasis. And away they start on a proud expedition across the rolling plain. The heart of the commander swells and bumps under his padded coat, and he puts his horse through a process of showy caracoling that both displays his own figure and delights an assembly already predisposed to admiration. How many a blushing girl at the rail-fence secretly wishes she could see her chosen one display himself to the multitude after a fashion like that! How many a hard-working mother, fresh from the butter-tray and the cheese-press, thinks that her son on that horse would surely look "the foremost man of all the world"! The crowds collect all along the lines, as they pass, inspired by the music that comes on with its rolling and screaming *crescendo.*

Nothing could be grander, either, in a small, human way, than the sight of those brilliant uniforms a-straddle of those richly caparisoned horses! I do not believe the armorers of the Middle-Ages ever set their iron dinner-pots on the skulls of Knights-errant one half so royally as our Colonel and his suite wear their heavy *chapeaus* of plush and plume; or that glaives and gauntlets of the days of romance and general tomfoolery ever surpassed those bright yellow buckskins that come half the way down the military arm. And the gilt bars across the breast, like a Venetian blind! the gilded epaulettes, with their trembling tendrils, on each shoulder! and the flowing sash, flowing plume, and flowing mane and tail of the horse of the commander!

To describe the "sham-fight" with which the day's exercises wind up, would require a pen like Homer's, (if he ever used such a thing,) so many are the heroes with portraits to be painted, and so stirring is the encounter between artillery and stump rifles and hickory sticks. The plain soon becomes a bank of smoke-clouds, which nothing but the return of welcome peace and sunrise can dissipate. Out of this blank-cartridge engagement the officers always manage to escape without wounds, and are found sitting on horses as sound of wind and as strongly inclined to repose as ever. The surgeon pays no sort of attention to *his* duties on the field; from which fact the affrighted females infer that none are wounded, let the dead number what they will.

Finally, the whole regiment is skilfully drawn up in the form of a hollow square, shutting in its officers with the chaplain much as cows are yarded in the country; and, when all is still, the "God of battles" is solemnly invoked on behalf of this yearly muster of inoffensive armed men; and then the closed wings unfold to let the cooped leaders out again.

The regiment is somehow got back, by hawing and geeing, into line, — the drums are briskly beaten a little while longer, — the Colonel takes another ride up and down the length of the rather serpentine column, — and, at last, from his seat in the saddle, the order is given to dismiss, and the companies march off each to its own rendezvous, firing a mild salute at the approaching sunset. And men and boys, women and girls, white, black, and yellow, reluctantly prepare to go home, and to bed as quick as they can get there.

This is the annual "training" of thirty years ago. We have passed through serious experiences since, in which the raw troops of the country pastures have nobly vindicated the fame of their Revolutionary ancestry before the country and the world.

THE COUNTY FAIR.

A MILD, hazy, dreamy day in early October. The place — the shire-town of the County, where the Courts are held. The hour — a very early one in the morning.

Cattle have been coming in, in droves, for some time, hurried forward by men in wagons and boys on foot who are dressed for the stirring events of the day. The tavern-doors are opened, and the landlords are out in their shirt-sleeves, sweeping the steps and the ground just before the windows. People are slowly and one by one awaking to the dawn and its new demands, up and down the village street. Select herds of stock straggle along through the town, from time to time, and file off to the grounds just behind, where they go into such quarters as may have been designated by the proper committees.

Presently a wagon, or two, rolls leisurely along, bringing a load of handsome poultry in its capacious body, — coops of geese, ducks, and hens of every known blood, breed, and variety. A colt comes whinnying at the foot of her dam, both of them to add to the day's attractions in the list of live-stock.

There is a sweet rural fragrance everywhere. You can even smell new-mown hay, in imagination, with the sight of the strings of jogging oxen and the sound of the herds of lowing cows. The sun comes over the street, at last, and the whole town — grass, trees, and houses — is steeped in the yellow glory of an autumnal morning.

By eight o'clock the crowds begin to gather everywhere. First, they group in little knots on the corners, and along down the sides of the street; and afterwards they get mixed up in a homogeneous mass. The chief centre of all attraction in the village is the town-house, where are to be seen the various articles of female ingenuity and industry, and all the untold products of flower and kitchen gardens; likewise, tempting specimens of bakery, of butter and cheese, and of all those other creature comforts that impart such a rich creaminess to the life of the generous farmer.

The one other point of attraction, to divide the honors of the day with the attention of the thousand spectators, is the "Show-Grounds."

To the *real* lover of rural sights and sounds, with an imagination to be inflamed and a sympathy to be excited by such things, this is the very place to which his feet turn at an early hour in the morning.

Pens are constructed of rough boards, ranging over an area of several acres. Tickets are tacked upon them, inscribed with the names of those who own the contents. You begin at the head of the row with some fine calves, bläting in your face and eyes as if they mistook you for a relative long absent. Next comes a pen of handsome red cows; then brindle; then clear red-and-white, grade cows, that are handsome enough to be of full blood; then bulls; then more cows; more calves; cows — cows — cows again, one, two, and three in a pen; pretty heifers, as pretty as ever graced a new name or a new cedar milk-pail; then sheep, — Leicester, Cotswolds, Southdown, and Merino, in various strains of crossing.

The sheep huddle timidly into the further corners of their pens, and look out through the crevices as if they wanted to ask the Committee when this tiresome pen-performance would be over. Their white and downy wool catches the eye for a long row of piney divisions; and then succeeds the department of swine. Our farmer friends believe in pork, even as, at the South, they return ever to their bacon. With a fair proportion of pork, cabbage, potatoes, and beans, they would get through the hardest winter, or the longest year, with almost the luxurious content of an early Roman Emperor; even old Heliogabalus could not have prided himself more loftily on his turbot and peacock sauce. The Hog used to be the guardian spirit of the New England farm, — so it might have been contended; for the population certainly worshipped him in all forms and on all occasions. The farmer could scarcely seat himself at his table without finding his old swine-friend there before him. We have changed that a little now, but not altogether; as the principles of physiology are more widely spread and become better understood, we may hope, all of us, to " return to our muttons."

But Piggy stands up and lies down in these pens at the Show, knee-deep in nice, clean straw, studying human nature by the help of that inquisitive little eye as it throngs past, and sometimes seeming perplexed — and with reason — to settle it whether himself or those who stir him up so unceasingly may be charged with the more genuine hoggishness. Strange as it is, everybody looks over the pens at the swine; and all the little boys of the country peep through the cracks at the white runts of pigs trying to hide in the straw, and squeak at them in mean and mimicking derision.

There is a ploughing-match on an open plain hard by, which the sturdy young farmers attend in numbers; for it is *the plough* that ushered in all the triumphs and rewards of the modern systems of agriculture. Fine yokes of oxen, clear red, descendants of the elegant creatures that hail from old Devonshire, stand about on the outer limits, and the Committee are examining their good points with due care and closeness. Then the few horses that are brought here are held all the while by grooms, and men pass along from one to the other, "talking horse" with more or less confidence, according to their tastes. The neighing and whinnying increases the confusion of sounds, and, mingled with the lowing of cattle and the bleating of sheep, brings out the spirit of rusticity to the utmost; one can realize, on the spot, the prettiest rural picture ever sketched in English poetry.

There is general bustle, very soon; the several Committees, with ribbons flying from their button-holes, are moving briskly from pen to pen, paper and pencil in hand, getting ready their reports and awards. The farmers have now brought their good wives and buxom daughters upon the ground, and they are ranging up and down the rows of enclosures and scanning with genuine interest every specimen of stock they contain. Do you suppose a bright country girl has not as quick an eye for a promising heifer, or a motherly milker, as she has for the sprucest young fellow who throws "sheep's-eyes" at her in meeting, and then comes to "sit up" with her of a Sunday evening?—or that, like the superb Europa herself, she may not regard the points of a noble bull with swelling admiration, and wish that a strain of that high blood were infused into the herd of milkers in her own father's yard? Our fair English ladies are at home just there; it was left for latter-day Yankees to touch a point of fastidiousness that lies a good way out of the reach of refinement itself.

The court-house, up-stairs and down, is crammed with the details of this annual display. Here centre mainly the industry and interests of the domestic department. Here you can stroll about at your leisure, jostled, of course, and jammed as you go, and inspect the handiwork of the wives and the daughters. It is spread out over tables and benches, arranged under glass coverings, hung against the walls, piled upon shelves, and suspended from the ceiling. It beautifies and enriches the whole place. If the show-grounds offer the attractions of *profits* to the eye of the observer, the hall and other rooms crowd the brain with suggestions of comfort, and plenty, and domestic luxury. All devices possible to execute in embroidery attract and delight the sight. Wonders of industrious ingenuity in the bed-quilt line hang, like choicest domestic tapestry, about the different rooms. Socks and stockings, soft enough to have been woven from the Golden Fleece, are displayed at several points of attraction ; and mittens, though not of the sort sometimes given by the girls, are on exhibition along with them. Butter and cheese, too, in the dairy department, arranged around so temptingly as that one can scarcely help slicing the neighboring loaves and spreading them *thick*, on the spot.

Soon after noon, when the appetites of the thousand or more comers have had a chance to get their edge a little taken off, the meeting-house — or church — begins to fill up with an expectant assembly. The influential ladies of the town are observed to show the way to the rest, and presently the people begin to flock in.

For Esquire Somebody, one of the greatest lawyers (not *farmers*) of the county, is going to address the committees and assembled citizens, on the topic which seems to engross the attention of all, that day. The house once fairly full, the orator, in personal charge of still another Committee, traverses the central aisle and climbs the stairs to the pulpit-box, whence he very soon proceeds to fulminate the thunders of his knowledge, and to flash the lightnings of his wit — a little rusty — upon the approving auditory below. Possibly, in imagination, he tries to realize what it would cost him, in vital resources, to exchange his own profession for that of the gentleman whose place this regularly is. At all events, he gives them a good Address, in the course of which ploughs and furrows, rhetoric and assertion, flattery and flummery, — considered only from the agricultural point, of course, — are adroitly mixed up. No matter, however, if "the ladies" are well pleased; and though he may know no more of agriculture practically than is contained in the term "boundary fence," yet if he do but praise the butter and cheese over at the hall, and talk beautifully on the influence of woman, with a little something about "fair hands" and "own vine and fig-tree," the harangue is esteemed a success, and the dignity of Agriculture is once more happily vindicated.

After this discourse, the reports of the various Committees are heard; and then it is, the heart of many a young farmer swells with deserved pride, to have it proclaimed to all the country round that he can beat the best of them at raising stock, or fattening swine, or guiding the plough across an even piece of greensward. Or the matrons grow a little red in the face, at hearing — exactly as they wished to — that their particular lot of butter and cheese bears off the year's palm; or the girls vainly try to hide their heads, to learn, in the presence of *that congregation*, that they have earned public praise and corresponding prizes for making bread that is as light as a sponge, knitted the evenest and softest stockings, and patched the prettiest bed-quilts. A vast deal of whispering and tittering may be heard over the church while this department of the prize-reading goes on; and, as for the disappointed ones, leave them alone to find good reasons enough, and plenty of them, for their defeat in this contest, which, happily, renders them none the less eager for another year's trial.

The usual resolutions are read and passed;

new committees are appointed for directing the next year's proceedings; and the assemblage disperses amid a hum of talk and general good humor. And then, one by one, parties begin to make up for home. It may be that they have come ten, twenty, or even more miles to this festival; they ride off gayly, satisfied with the pleasures and profits of the day, content if they reach their homes in the damp coolness of a lovely autumn evening.

The remainder of the afternoon is devoted to the sale of such cattle and other stock as their owners are willing to dispose of, and to the gathering up of property previous to getting it back to the farms on which it belongs. The scenes on the show-grounds are then extremely interesting. More of the real farmer feeling breaks out, as if all were met at an informal meeting; and the swapping and jockeying make the occasion as lively as any of the Fair Days in the rural districts of Old England. Not until long after the usual hour at night is the town street still again, parties being given at the dwellings of some of the leading citizens, and the taverns unable to be quiet, with their company, till every item of the day's doings has been thoroughly discussed.

THE COUNTRY MINISTER.

THEY have none of the fine clergymen to be found in novels, among the hard hills of New England. Such poetry as has been thrown around the calling in other countries does not belong to it there. It is, instead, the most actual and outright prose possible.

Times have changed about very strangely since the days of our fathers, — that we know; and, along with the times, the relations between pastor and people also. A genial and facetious clergyman of Massachusetts remarked, in the course of a telling speech at a horse-show, that the horse was a truly noble animal, and a nice piece of property for a minister; for he verily believed the time was close at hand when it would be necessary for ministers to *settle* on horseback!

The old-fashion, old-school, patriarchal, positive, dogmatic, yet benevolent ministers who used to maintain their fixed positions from one end of the land to the other, are nearly all passed away; and none come forward to supply their places, simply because the condition of society requires a new order of men. These were stern men and godly; puritan and primitive; ascetic in their habits and forbidding in their mien, yet as playful as kittens at heart, praying to God morning and evening that they might be kept innocent of all guile. They were established, with their families, on broad and fertile acres, — and still, the acres were as likely to prove sterile as fertile. They domiciled in huge rectangular houses, with low ceilings and rambling rooms; sat at boards laden with substantial cheer, and garnished with goodly rows of children; and kept their horse apiece, and their cow or two, and their oxen sometimes, — a yoke or so, — with whose patient help they ploughed their stubborn glebe in the springs.

Theirs was a day and generation by itself. They were the Popes of their isolated parishes, — the Clements and Hildebrands of all the country round. Beside the doctor and the lawyer of the place, no one knew so much as "our minister." Indeed, not even *they* were at all times admitted to an equality in the popular esteem with himself. The little girls and boys were taught to fear his frown, and to feel eternally grateful for so much as a ray of his benignant, but strictly conscientious, smile. When he walked down the road with that solemn tread, the females would hurry to the front windows and summon all within their hearing to come and see the minister go by. They seemed to believe the very atmosphere around him was a sort of "glory." Even the earth on which he left the print of his substantial soles they esteemed half sacred by reason of his tread. What he divided of the Word among them on the Sabbaths, they accepted with thanks and without the thought of venturing a question. His Scripture commentaries were received as final, and quite beyond the disturbance of human criticism. His definition of the doctrines he so stoutly enforced was the beginning and end of true theology, — the Alpha and Omega of biblical truth.

Outside of the old Romish Church herself, it would be difficult to find an individual in any age, who so perfectly personated, by his influence and force of character, the almost unlimited power of its priests. It was genuine Theocracy. While eschewing and combatting, and denouncing and defying that Church, with all the rigor, and aroused energy, and passion of his rugged nature, he at the same time, and in his own way, illustrated most strangely the powers and peculiarities against which he was so fervently praying and contending.

Such were the ministers of the Oldtime. They had the spirit of *fight* in them, and plenty of it. They were bred up to make a show of pluck, as well in the pulpit as out; and could flourish a sword, or handle a musket; or lead a forlorn hope, — some of them, — as well as many more who cut such figures on the page of history. They took their stand, whether on religion or politics, and vigorously defended it. Not a foot was yielded to the assaulting enemy, whether human or satanic; they would sooner throw inkstands in return, as did unyielding Luther. The last thing they would do was give quarter; that was a favor they neither asked nor accepted for themselves, but fought until fighting was of no further use, one party only being left for future operations. In such habits of mind, it is true that the gentler and more Christlike qualities of the Soul were not always called out; but the work to be done — rough pioneer work as it was — was not of the sort for sentimentalists to take in hand, or for lily-white rhapsodists and rhetoricians, with smoothly ironed bands beneath their chins. These brave and sturdy old ministers, with their hearts of oak, had rough work before them; and they did it thoroughly and well.

But a race like that passed away with the times that demanded its services. A new race trode in its footsteps, inheriting all its vigorous and independent qualities of character, fully as dogmatic in its opinions and as deeply rooted in its prejudices, yet with a degree of flexible adaptiveness, yielding to the changing temper and custom of the times, though claiming just the same show of veneration from its entire parishes, and seeking to impose the same servile fear on all the little boys and girls that came in its way.

And still another, and another class has followed; in some respects mellowing, and, as it were, humanizing with each advance, but in its main qualities of character copying with a rigid spirit of veneration the very traits, speech, and manners of those ancient and time-honored men, whose names are engraven more enduringly than in brass.

The modern New England minister is hardly the minister, or the man, of the Old School. While he lacks — and knows it — the vigorous energy of the latter, and is wanting in that fearless independence which never quailed in an emergency, he nevertheless seeks to compensate for the loss by mechanical conformity with a few antiquated manners and customs, — such as pertain to the cutting of his hair, the hue and tie of his cravat, the shape of his boots, the solemn deep-soundings of his voice, and perhaps the rigid style of his family living. Many a man will keep the form, though the life went out of it long ago. To him who can penetrate beneath the surface, forms have almost ceased to offer any meaning.

—— But all country ministers are not to be set down in these matters upon the same footing. There are differences, according to location. At the West, customs go for less than almost anywhere else ; but in the Eastern States, and in New England especially, they must be studied in connection with the people and the prosperity around them. There are "Sunnysides" and "Shadysides" everywhere among the valleys of New England ; and within the walls of country parsonages — where, indeed, they have any parsonages at all — stories are yet to be written, — tragedies, some of them, — that will hold the attention of the most thoughtless skater over the surface of print.

Nowadays, they go to their parishes young, — that is, as soon as they obtain their licenses at the Schools, or whenever they have taken to themselves blooming and blessing wives as companions on the journey. They first preach a few times in a place, are perhaps liked, learn how much was paid the last minister, and close the bargain and settle down. From that day forward, themselves and their youthful wives become public property; their finest sensibilities are a sort of highway for inconsiderate tongues to walk and wag over. They give a good day's study to the quarters which the parish has provided for them, get acquainted with the deacons, find their way as fast as they can over their extended parish, hurry together their several articles of household economy, and at last report of themselves, and try actually to feel, that they are settled.

For a time, how lonely! If father and mother could but drop in, some pleasant afternoon, and take an early tea with them, — how much sooner those strange rooms, with their stranger echoes, would seem cheerful! All faces are new to them. They cannot yet tell who come from pure friendliness, and who just to see their "new things." Between a state of half sadness and one of joy, their hearts are for a time divided, and light and shadow long alternate across their path.

Every country minister has peculiar experiences; the country is not so monotonous in this respect as many persons would infer. Various in various localities, they are essentially alike, too, or at least essentially related. The deacons in one town are not likely to be always the same with the deacons in the town adjoining. The social temper here is not necessarily the same with the social temper there. In one place, the people are perhaps a little inclined to social gayety, or what would be esteemed such outside their own bailiwick; in the very next town to it, the public face may be drawn down to a longitude which only skilful navigators can take the measure of.

Generally, the minister keeps a horse; sometimes a cow; but always a handful of hens. He must have something to pet. He and his wife take infinite delight with their poultry, and so do the little ones, especially at the time of the Spring hatchings. The cow proves herself a blessed creature for the little folks, and, in fact, more than half keeps the family. And they are all so fond of patient "mooley," too, and love to see the white streams of her milk churning into the pail at night, standing and patting her sides while she solemnly chews her cud and contemplates the advantages of being the *minister's cow!*

A horse is hardly so common a piece of property among country ministers, though all of them would like well enough to own one. He costs more money than the cow, in the first place; and unless some man of means happens to be kind enough, or the minister himself has married well enough, or by hook and by crook laid aside enough, after teaching school and purchasing his library with the proceeds, to buy such an animal outright, — his stall in the barn is crammed with dried cornstalks in winter, and contains an old wheelbarrow and a rusty stove or two in summer.

Some parishes — we could put our finger on one such, at this moment — would much prefer *not* to have their minister own a horse; it gives him too wide a margin for operating independently of *them.* He can thus reach the cars too readily to satisfy some who would like to domineer over even his means of locomotion. His poor wife can take a much-needed airing across the country with too little trouble. He will himself be apt to spend too liberally of his time on the road, at the harness-maker's, in the cheery blacksmith's shop, and calling around on brother ministers in neighboring parishes. To whom, if not to his own people, does his time belong? Has not each and every one of them an interest as abiding in his hours and days as in the meeting-house itself, or the red school-house at the fork of the road? In their unrelenting estimate, is he not as accountable to them for the way he spends his time as they are, in other public directions, for the way they spend theirs?

To write two long sermons each week is double what any man of intellectual gifts and genuine spiritual attainments ought ever to think of attempting. Lectures for an evening each week he generally appoints, too; and he is expected to lend his presence and influence at all the bees, sociables, and society meetings that, during the winter at least, divide the week into two unmistakable halves. If a single family in the wide-spread parish chances to be even once overlooked in the annual visit of the minister, he is very sure to hear of it in a strain of emphasis not soon forgotten. The people of his parish are not so delicately organized in the region of their sensibilities, or so forbearing in the use of their mother tongue, as to keep back anything of that sort from *him.* If he errs, they make a point to let him know it; he is not to think he was invited among them to point out *their* errors; the *digito monstrari* lies altogether on their side.

Little enough time, therefore, all things considered, do country ministers have left in which to cultivate a taste for books and general literature. In a good many up-country parishes, it is esteemed rather effeminate to pay much attention to letters, and discourses that are guilty of the least literary finish are held to be emasculate and ineffective. The people not only want the Word, but they want it as hard and dry as a navy biscuit. Neither the deacons nor the old women believe in mental culture; they ask for the raw staple of brains, without any fine spinning to it. To confess a love for the poets, those masters of melody and divine philosophy, is to betray a weakness not apt to be overlooked in estimating the soundness of a sermon. There are parishes, and not all of them so remote, either, in which if a minister were to be *known* to offer a quotation from a favorite author, even giving credit as he proceeds, a woe would rest heavily on his local reputation forever after. His discourses would never again be entirely his own; he would be charged with borrowing even his language; and the deacons would set him down as but a copy of something, or somebody, he had been indiscreet enough to tell them about, — either a book, or an author, they cannot clearly comprehend.

—— In the family of the country minister, however, may often be found — especially if his life have the flavor of the ancient times in it — some of that sweetest contentment which comprises about all there is of earthly happiness, and which never fails to attract the admiring envy of all who behold it. A genuinely happy family is not so common a sight in these latter days as that people do not stop to study the phenomenon. Around the cheerful family table sit the sons and daughters, coming forward to be ornaments in society, and chief ornaments already in the harmonious household. Love sits at the bottom and the top, and Love runs all the way through. How dutiful — how affectionate — how obedient! We can here realize the happy figure of the "sitting beneath one's own vine and fig-tree," and lovely indeed is the vision to eyes unaccustomed to beholding it.

Perhaps the city clergyman does know more, because he sees more, of human nature, and of the human heart under varied and strangely contrasting circumstances, — but the country minister is drawn nearest to Nature, the common mother. If he is not so intellectual as his city brother, he is more spiritual. He meditates his discourses in the pleasant fields, and out upon the farm-lands which stretch broad and far their limits. The fresh airs of the woods and ferny pastures should drift through his sermons, and make them fragrant and reviving to all who hear them spoken. And the closeness of the pastoral relation in sickness, in death, in baptism, in the office of marriage, is something not so well known to his brethren in the cities, who lay their hands upon the throbbing hearts of their people but seldom. All the associations of country life are calculated to make the offices and experiences of ministers settled in rural parishes distinct from the corresponding offices of their brethren of the large towns. The unhappy poet of Olney meant volumes more than he could have read himself, when he cast the well-known phrase, — "God made the country, but Man made the town."

The country minister, like the country schoolmaster — his congener, is of necessity a trifle less pliant in his manners than his municipal brother; and one reason for it is, there is so much more *looking* than *doing*, so much more *criticism* than *being*, all around him. The argus eyes that watch him from Sunday to Sunday, and the voluble and well-trained tongues that take verbal measure, with such fearful accuracy, of whatever he says and does, — like rows of batteries ever ready to belch their fires upon him, — compel a sort of constraint in spite of himself. Hence his stilted ways, and overshot style of expression; he is aware of it, and secretly laments it, — but his fate is upon him and he can do nothing. He rarely unbends, or "lets himself out," for there is never an occasion for him to do it, and nobody with whom he may. Unconsciously to himself he has the behavior of a person beset with spies, — though possibly harmless ones, — and feels that all his phrases are translated with as much literalness, and into as true polyglot, as those of Holy Writ itself. The female portion of the parish are inquisitive, in spite of their efforts to seem otherwise; and they cannot propose to perform kind and gentle offices for the minister's family, without betraying the instinct that refuses to be concealed. They have so grown into the habit of taking toll as they go along.

—— Reviewing the whole ground, therefore, it would be hard to say that the condition of the minister settled in the country *is* just the pleasantest which might be imagined by a young licentiate. Of really tough and tussocky obstacles he has his full share to contend with. In every conceivable way is his patience put to the test. So many little trials is he summoned to endure, and endure in silence. So much gossip — so much envy — so much jealousy in respect of his family — and he is so often headed off at the very point where he should have been helped, — his place sometimes becomes a burden which he cannot carry, and his term of real usefulness comes to an end. Finally, and worst of all, there is the danger of a young man's relapsing into the very customs he so positively dislikes. To see fine and fresh powers slowly coating with the palsying gum of old up-country observances, prejudices, and whimsicalities, — to behold a young man, full of ardor and promise, falling gradually away into the habit of insensibility and actual induration, by reason simply of some lack, or else of the positive coarseness, of those among whom his lot is cast, — is something to make the heart feel sad indeed. To be sure, not all country parishes are with an influence like this; yet there are enough to make themselves a reproach to religion, and their ministers practically useless by becoming so thoroughly unhappy.

THE COUNTRY DOCTOR.

OLD Dr. Twogood I knew very well. He was the sort of man for everybody *to* know, who could. Fond of a story, attached to his few rows of well-used books, his parish of friends, and his steady, dock-tailed mare, I honestly believe no man ever took life, as life goes with us all, more humorously, comfortably, and contentedly than he. Like the minister, everybody knew him well, or, like the sign-post on Sundays, everybody consulted him. Rotund, red-faced, and ever disposed to be jolly, he was the sample for lean and Cassius-like patients to copy after so far as they could. They needed but to have a good look at his happy face, to give the right turn to the whole list of their complaints. There might, indeed, have been some miraculous element in it all,— like the touching of garment hems in olden times, or the going down into healing pools to wash.

I think there are few men so placed in the

social arrangement, and especially in that of the country neighborhood, that their influence can be made as general and genial as that of the regular physician. The family doctor is the one privileged visitor. He has the key to our doors and hearts. He dispenses a great deal more healing by his manner than by his less intelligible prescriptions. What passes his oracular lips often works better service than what he writes down in abbreviated Latin. The country physician, in the nature of things, is drawn by very close and confidential relations to his patients. He has a work to do peculiarly his own. He is emphatically a "family man." His sympathies are all more or less domestic, and all his aims centre, or appear to do so, in Home.

Scott describes one of these human benefactors in the "Chronicles of the Canongate," in these words: — "There is no creature in Scotland that works harder, and is more poorly requited than the country doctor, unless perhaps it may be his horse. Yet the horse is, and indeed must be, hardy, active, and indefatigable, in spite of a rough coat and indifferent condition; and so you will often find in his master, under a blunt exterior, professional skill and enthusiasm, intelligence, humanity, courage and science."

While practising at his profession, he carries on a farm as well; generally showing as fine fruits and as large vegetables as any other cultivator in town, and keeping the most liberal share of each to bestow upon his friend, the minister, along in the sunny days of autumn. A better garden than Dr. Twogood kept and dressed, I think I never knew nor saw. There were no vegetables, whether common or rare, which he had not industriously laid under tribute for family service, through the instrumentality of his little patch of land. He hoed and grubbed in it by the hour, all by himself,—planting his beans, sowing his radishes and peas, pulling or scraping the weeds, picking bugs most patiently from his cucumber vines, and stirring the soil where it needed mellowing.

I never left off envying him the pleasure he took among his apple-trees, in that pretty orchard which made regular avenues across the slope back of his house, and thence down into the meadows. In that spot he appeared entirely happy. It was to me a convincing illustration of what I had an intuitive knowledge of before, that our simplest and least costly pleasures are worth most to us, and that the memory of them abides longest. The Doctor looked to me, in that particular spot, like the lord of the land; or, perhaps, like some jolly poet among his trees, familiarizing himself with the bent of their disposition, one by one, — nodding to them whenever they seemed to nod, — passing his hands in a friendly way up and down their stems, — pulling over their boughs toward him, — and plunging his eyes into the dense banks of green with which they made the landscape beautiful. The whole of it suggested to me the picture of the true life; it seemed so simple, so sweet, and so wholesome.

If a man should run in to ask the Doctor to come over and see his wife just as quick as he could, or to take in hand one of his children who had been stuffing with under-ripe cherries, or currants, or apples, he would very likely find him — if at all — in a lazy posture in his great office-chair, feet piled upon the table or braced against the jamb, hands folded with an air of permanency across his abdomen, and countenance prepared either to dissolve in smiles or break up in a horse-laugh, just as circumstances might seem to direct. That bit of a room, which he styled his "office," had seen a deal of medicinal experience in its day. Its atmosphere was heavy with the fragrance of boluses and gallipots. Plasters and surgical ingenuities lay rather promiscuously around. The windows were heavy with dust and curtained with cobwebs; and as for the floor, it was worn bare of carpet and paint with the shuffle and tread of heavily booted feet.

—— We all went in there one Sunday afternoon, just after tea. The old Doctor did n't happen to be in the room at the moment, but he soon came roystering along in his jolly manner from another room, where he said his wife had prevailed on him to go through the form of taking tea.

"And now, come," said he; "I believe we 've got a little something or another left on the table; and if we have n't, I 'm certain there 's something in the cupboard! So come — come right along; and just see for yourselves how much healthier 't is to live in a doctor's house than in some others!"

He enjoyed as sound digestion as a man could; hence, of course, his remarkable and uninterrupted flow of spirits. An observant old physician of Boston once said, that he could tell almost any man's creed by the state of his liver. Had it been proposed to apply this test to Dr. Twogood, it would have been found that a more orthodox, sound-at-heart, and thoroughly *religious* man nowhere enjoyed existence. It must have been owing, much of it, to his excellent digestion — very simple recipe for so placid and summer-morning like a disposition.

Riding about the country, and driving over the rough lanes and stony roads and grassy by-ways which he and his trusty beast knew so well, the Doctor became a feature — though not a very fixed one — in the rural landscape. He invariably rode in a narrow, high-shouldered, selfish-looking sulky, — some persons were ill-natured enough to say that he might not be asked to give a body a lift on the road. But Dr. Twogood was not the man to want an excuse for doing a selfish deed; he kept his sulky because it was easier for his faithful horse to carry him so, — because he had the floor exactly fitted to the transportation of his instruments and medicine-chest, — and, finally, because it was soonest got into and out of; reasons enough to satisfy the sourest grumbler. The old sulky was one of the well-understood institutions of the country neighborhood; jogging and creaking across the roads, jolting over the rocks and loose stones, trundling softly down the reaches of green turf that lined the old highways, and rolling and rattling at last up to the Doctor's door with an air of consequence which best betokened the true character of its inmate and owner.

The old horse, and the old carriage, which a man is in the habit of using every day, at length wears as much significance as one can find in the features, the walk, the dress, or the speech of the man himself; and that may stand for a reason why I have thus gone a little out of my way, taking my reader by the buttonhole, as it were, to treat in a semi-confidential style of the Doctor's sulky. It was as much the Doctor's self as his overcoat was, or his hat, or his laugh. Had you seen only that in the street, the horse drowsily dropping his head upon his knees, you would have been quite ready to say you had seen the Doctor himself.

—— But the most unaccountable thing is, what leads men of like profession to so fall out with one another. They are all guilty of it, in every profession known. The ministers quarrel, (don't try to make me believe they don't!) and are jealous of one another, and go off and say sour things one of the other, and sometimes refuse the bow of recognition in the streets. And the lawyers disagree on principle and habit both, to say nothing of interest, as any one may see for himself by paying a visit to the nearest court-room. Authors, too, are a quarrelsome race, — *irritabile genus*, — and fall into cat-and-dog practices, feeling that not to be praised is only worse than to hear their brethren well spoken of. And so through the list.

Even Dr. Twogood, kind and genial philosopher that he was, never was guilty of loving the other Doctor over at Seesaw — Dr. Plasther — any too well. Not a whit of friendship was wasted between them. They seemed born to dwell on different planets. So heartily did Dr. Twogood hate the other, Samuel Johnson, who liked above all things a sturdy hater, would have taken him to his arms. Could he have annihilated him with his breath alone, poor Plasther would long before have quit existence.

Whenever they met upon the cross-roads, as they sometimes did, each pursuing his way to the dwellings of his own patients, they saw nothing but the trees and stone walls before them; and these they looked at with intense attention. They never exchanged salutes, — even professional ones. If both chanced to be summoned to a consultation on the same case, of course they fell to hurling sharp-cornered words at one another if it could n't be helped; but it was in a very shying manner. They bolstered up none of their nouns with choice adjectives, and cushioned none of their epithets with soft adverbs; but they dealt in marrowy verbs, solid substantives, and very energetic pronouns. What was particularly noticeable, nearly all these latter parts of speech were *personal* pronouns. What passed from one to the other was as direct as a musket-ball, and could as readily have been mistaken in its meaning.

The most fun occurred — if there can be fun where matters are so serious in their consequences — when one was called to attend a family where the other could do no more, or which had lost faith in him. It was worth belonging to the anxious family itself, to witness the phenomenon. The rival doctor would come stalking in, and exclaim in a tone of authority before taking his seat, —

"You 've had Plasther here?"

"Yes, Doctor. But we don't think he understands the case. He said he had done all he could, — and so we sent for *you!*"

"Oho!" bawled the Doctor. "Then after finding out he 's a fool, you hurry over after *me*, just to let me know you don't think *me* one! A fine way to give me your opinion of *me*, by sending for *him!* I'd a mind not to come at all! I'd a notion of *letting* you suffer awhile, just to show you how good 't is!"

They sometimes made an effort to pacify him, either by offering a clean confession of their fault, or by inventing some little family excuses, — which were good so far as they went, and to a certain extent baffled the scrutiny and defied the objections of the Doctor.

Once mollified, however, he would calmly take his seat by the side of the patient, and proceed in the mechanical way to feel the pulse and study the tongue; after which, in rather stronger language than before, he fell to lamenting the rashness and wrong-headedness of *some* people, — and then to hope they would manage to get the scales off their eyes while *he* lived. The scene usually terminated with the Doctor's return to a normal and pleasanter state of feeling; in fact, he actually felt better for having been ruffled. Once well rid of his surplus bile, — whatever it might have been in quantity, — he became more companionable than ever.

Dr. Twogood furnished more than a fair average specimen of the country doctor. They are not all of them such easy souls as he, nor so full, even up to the chin, with the milk of human kindness. Few could style themselves so thoroughly domestic, or would know how to get so much pleasure out of their fruit orchards, their cattle, their pigs, and their poultry. Still, making due allowance here and due allowance there, they are, as a class, fond of the same sorts of pleasures. and inclined to the same class of recreative occupations. With all their drugs and pills, their preparations and tinctures, their bleedings and boluses, they form a most excellent class of citizens by themselves. Some of them are called coarse, and deservedly; they would be thought out of the reach of ordinary human sympathy. Such are the men who will seat you in a chair opposite, and fall to descanting on the pulseless heart of some person which they have just been dissecting, or on the moans and groans of some poor fellow who has lost a limb under their surgical knife and saw. We are glad these do not represent the profession. It is bad enough that there are so many of them.

In rural communities, the Doctor and his influence form an important element. You can ill afford to come into the country and overlook *him*. He dwells in a house as imposing as the minister's, or the lawyer's; these three houses, like the three men who inhabit them, form the chief exceptions to the group of roofs and chimneys, and may be allowed to impart a character to the whole. If a stranger enters the village, he is pointed to one of these three houses to begin with. From these he forms his idea of the place.

The habits and calling of a country doctor are not, perhaps, invested with as much interest as are those of the country lawyer, — yet they are distinct and noticeable. There stands his little office, — either a little box by itself, or a room set apart in his own dwelling. There is his old horse, trundling the respectable chaise, or sulky, behind him. There is his garden, and his orchard; and there stretch his modest outlands, for which he is as much to be envied as those whose longer titles form the larger part of the town records. He is one of the genuinely "solid men" of the place. His influence rills through the whole community. His advice is more sought after even than the minister's; certainly more than the lawyer's, for the latter makes a practice of *charging* for his.

These genial, jovial, domestic old doctors deserve more than the mention of mere words. They are our sterling men, props of the social edifice. In times of trial, they show that fibre of genuine courage which, in men of other callings, does not always make its appearance. I duly respect and honor them; some of them I could love. In spite of ipecac and emetics, blue pills and blister plasters, tourniquets and surgical saws, I cannot help my attachment for them, one and all. So intimately are science and the commonest common-sense mixed in their characters, it is ten to one that, before the world looks for it, it will catch a ray of light from a quarter generally thought dark and unpromising. A good country doctor, of the real old stamp and style, is, in truth, no such ordinary man. Not many grown men and women of the neighborhood, but owe him all thanks for the prolongation of their very unsatisfactory baby existence.

THE COUNTRY LAWYER.

IT so happens that my impressions of country 'squires date back in my early youth; and, to be candid, I cannot exactly say if I was possessed chiefly of a dislike or a fear of them all.

At this moment there rises in my mind's eye the great legal functionary of the little town of Follifog. In his little box of an office he sits in his arm-chair, of a summer afternoon, his feet fastened to the window-sill, his thumbs hooked in the armholes of his waistcoat, and his firm-set head as full of wisdom as an egg is of meat. If a client happens to be sharing the hour with him, he is either talking in that resonant tone which so impresses itself on all his clients' minds, or the brazen echoes of his professional laugh are reverberating up and down the village street.

He rejoices in that voice of his, which is so hard and loud, esteeming it a gift, by whose help he impresses his personal power upon clients and opponents alike. When he rises in court to wrangle and argue, it is with a deliberateness which few men can parallel. The sweet and bitter cud of legal lore he chews without cessation. Fortified within the entrenchments of professional dignity, he sallies out only when he feels very sure of bringing back the enemy captive. All the little boys look up to him in wonder, remembering what a hand he has had in sending off thieves and drunkards and otherwise questionable characters to the county lock-up. Mothers have a habit of looking askance at him on Sundays, while he is at such pains to make a display of wristbands to the congregation, wondering, perhaps, if he is really like other men, or if he possesses no more than a vulgar-fractional nature, about equally divided between the horse and the human, — griffinish and fabulous. None of them are fond of thinking he would prove a match for their daughters; and yet, too many of them would actually be proud of such a connection, even if they could foresee the unsatisfactory lives their girls would lead in consequence.

There are some few persons, and particularly in country towns, who imagine it a great lift to be a lawyer. They regard this character as the Jupiter Tonans of the rural Olympus. They associate all that is great and worthy in the State with his occupation. He, of all the rest, is the one man who attends to the business of everybody else. He is as handy at private as at public affairs. He draws up wills for dying persons — has a hand in the settlement of estates — throws his professional guardianship around the orphans and fatherless — becomes the trustee of property of all descriptions and values — manages delicate questions arising between the different members of the same family — improves the slender estates of widows and maiden ladies — attends the justice courts, those rural standards and institutes of law and order — helps employ a teacher for the Academy — and is sometimes an active member of that very important body known as the Church Committee. There is, in fact, no office which the village advocate and attorney is not qualified to fill. Let it be never so trifling and inconsiderable, he will manage to invest it with such pomp and circumstance of learned phraseology as shall make it seem scarcely less important and dignified than the Presidency itself. It is indeed a wonder, what a faculty a country lawyer has of extracting the very essence of dignity out of some kinds of occupation, in themselves so pitiful and mean.

In the same town of Follifog lived and practised, too, Squire Brigham. The Squire was one of the reputed Solons of the place. He was a man very generally "looked up to," by foe as well as by friend. Aside from the doctor and the minister, no one was popularly reckoned wiser than he. In the stores and at the tavern men listened to him with eagerness, and felt grateful to catch the very drippings from the eaves of his wisdom — without a fear of being asked for a fee. He could stand and face people in church with a settled assurance that was worth a fortune to any lawyer; and few were the eyes which could wrestle with his, and not catch a sudden fall.

In his profession, no man was ever known to be more stirring than Squire Brigham. Everybody knew that, to their cost. Numbers who had gone to law under his lead for "damages" were quite ready to admit that they got them. By the force of his energy and the persuasiveness of his eloquence, he had managed to secure plentiful emoluments, and was — at the particular time I speak of — on the high road to public office and favor. Long ago had the popular voice pronounced him a "smart" lawyer, which means whatever you please. What the popular *heart* might have chosen to say of him, — supposing it possessed so "miraculous" an organ as a tongue, — would not so well suit this present purpose to repeat. He occupied as fine a house as any man in town already. He "stood high" with the inhabitants, and exchanged familiar calls with the minister's family; and in the days when the ministers of sequestered towns in New England were virtually Popes in their little realms, this one fact was a sure guaranty of respectability, if not an actual passport to local eminence.

The lawyer's house stood behind a couple of silvery sycamores, scarcely more stately than himself, that imparted a mansion-like appearance to the dwelling itself; whilst within the cincture of its white filagree fence throve shrubs and flowers enough to have made the heart of any country lawyer as soft as a woman's, a poet's, or a story-teller's. The front walk was of broad and clean flagging-stones, which was a luxury very few of the householders round about could well afford. A huge lilac-bush stood beneath either front window, and furnished, in the season of flowering, fragrance for the whole length of the street; while it unhappily led not a few little boys, on their way to Sabbath-school, into desperate bogs of temptation, from a desire to snap off spikes of the royal purple blossoms and stick them in their button-holes. Snow-balls, too, were growing in immense clusters in that yard; and, here and there, a hollyhock, a bunch of pinks, and a screen of morning-glory vines before a window.

But Squire Brigham is a representative of the "upper class" of country lawyers; Mr. Jenkins is several grades below him. He — Jenkins — is a much younger man. He has n't yet taken a wife. He is not allowed, by the adjudication of public sentiment, to do a good many things that a man like Judge Bingham — for example — can do with perfect impunity.

He sits — Jenkins still — in an office with the proportions of a snug hen-coop; and all around him busy spiders weave their webs for giddy flies, suggesting the meshes he is all the time weaving in his brain to entangle unsuspecting men and women. The new calf-bound law books that give his shelves an imposing air, and litter his table as with an appearance of business, call up visions of dead-and-buried lawsuits, — ghosts of long-departed plaintiffs and defendants who will never enter the legal tilt-yard more, — estates rent into ravelings by the lingual dexterity of cunning and voluble lawyers, — together with a body of established principles of law and equity, that leave all parties to an issue as much in the fog as before the attorneys and judges conspired to develop such confusion.

—— Justice Courts furnish one of the staple entertainments of a country town, or village. On rainy days, they are peculiarly interesting. The male part of the population is in a state of what is styled "high cockolorum." On the occasions when these are held, there is leisure enough for everybody, no matter what his trade or occupation. The men can't work out in the fields; the tanners would hardly keep dry around their sloppy vats in the oozy yards; there is no wood to be hauled to the back-door; and the only talk at the store is of approaching Court.

This is held either in the open bar-room, or the more spacious hall above stairs. In this particular Court it is where Mr. Jenkins awakes to a sense of his individual glory. In the frowning presence of the Justice of the Peace, and of that miscellaneous tribunal whose applause he craves with such eagerness, he browbeats, cross-examines, and habitually bullies timid witnesses, — male and female, — and returns to his coop of an office after the day's work is done, secure of the fame for which he strives and about which he fondly dreams.

If you could but *behold* him in that noticeable hall of justice, thus invested with the high sense of his own importance, gazing so vacantly over the crowd of staring spectators, running his hand so carelessly through his hair, hurling his high-keyed interrogatories at the abashed witnesses, watching every chance to convulse the too ready auditory with laughter, bold and brazen in his address, rarely, if ever, thrown off his guard, compelling the village Shallow behind the table to shrink into the proportions of submissive inferiority, running over at the mouth with legal phrases and the technical lingo of legal instruments, reclining entirely upon his own dignity, assured that, of all the rest, he is nearly the largest toad in the entire town puddle, and, in fine, quite satisfied with his cause, his audience, himself, and his prospects for the future!

The character of the country lawyer's occupations cannot, of course, yield any large share of refined social and domestic enjoyment. He cannot well afford, from the very nature of the case, to put his sensibilities out to school. He lives, and must hope to live, chiefly upon the

16

unhappy differences and discords of the limited world around him. The more his neighbors fall out, the better it is for him. He watches for new chances for a lawsuit as sharply as a cat waits at a rat-hole. As for the finer sentiments of local friendship, he can ill afford to indulge them. They are luxuries which cost too much.

—— This is the thorough-bred pettifogger. The work he performs is small drudgery, at the most. It may be necessary, much of it; but that necessity even does not redeem it from the imputation of meanness. Yet, if such a reflection ever stings him, he is consoled with the thought that he is pursuing a "profession" — pursuing it just as much greater men have done before him, and with a brand of ambition blazing somewhere in his heart. He is struggling for a name; scanning the political horizon, from time to time, as a mariner comes up on deck and studies the clouds; living among, and altogether *upon*, his fellow-citizens, yet not *of* them, in any true and hearty sense.

He is in the full blaze of his glory in the County Court term. If he cannot bring a case before that court, he is esteemed but a "scant pattern" of a lawyer. It is at that bar the country lawyer is in full feather. The quiet little shire town of the county, at these court terms, overflows with rustic humanity, come to look after its own and into everybody's else business. The accommodations of the pair of rival taverns are put to their severest strain. Through the days, all the stalls in the stables and the stands in the horse-sheds are occupied. The judge, lawyers, and witnesses, — saying nothing of the hangers-on who attend court as regularly as they do a muster, — have monopolized stables and dormitories. The town carries its head erectly now. Writs, summons, capiases, copies, mittimuses, executions, and the whole of that sort of legal paper-work, fly from hand to hand like ballots at a tight election. Sleepy crowds stand or sit through the proceedings in the court-room, or discuss, out of doors, the merits of the cases and the lawyers, as they come on. There is a stream of male and female witnesses, going up and down stairs; and the lawyers are marching them in and out of lobbies and anterooms for preparatory drill in the science of giving in testimony. It looks as if large boys were playing at trials, and not altogether like serious men, transacting serious business.

—— The country lawyer, however, is not what he was in the days of our fathers; and he knows it as well as any one else. His glory has in a great degree departed. Since imprisonment for debt became obsolete, and debtors otherwise grew to be the masters rather than the slaves of their creditors, his business and corresponding importance have shrivelled and disappeared. Though still as great a character as any other in the town, he finds his sway clipped in both wings. He falls in with a man, now and then, who knows about as much good law as he does. He mistrusts that somehow intelligence has got abroad,—that the dam has been breached in some weak place, and the long-pent waters are overflowing the whole land.

Hence, he has been induced to take a lesson or two in modesty, and in forbearance also. He sees that it is well to pay a little more respect to popular wishes than the men of the old school were in the habit of doing. It may be a fact, he thinks, that men are growing more *human* and less *legal*. They are beginning to look to other methods of persuasion than those harsh and unsympathetic ones which are comprised in the technicalities, the musty learning, and the mandatory spirit of that grand science which goes, the world over, by the name of LAW.

THE COUNTRY POSTMASTER.

A COUNTRY Post-Office, as a general matter, is simply a country store, with some odd corner railed off for secresy, if not security. Anybody can go around behind there, if he is so fortunate as to be in the confidence — social or political — of the village Postmaster. It is chiefly the women who step up to that desk timidly and doubtingly, as if asking a favor, — or sidle along, as girls do, and inquire for a letter in the softest whisper, lest even their names should be pronounced aloud in that public presence. To the rude boys the place is *caviare.* For them alone is the iron rail spiked down so rigidly into the counter, — to keep off trousers' stuffs and heavy swinging boots.

Kegs and barrels — nail-boxes and soap-boxes — customers and letter-writers — men and boys — women and dogs — the box-stove and the department letter-boxes — are all mingled at the post-office establishment with picturesque incongruity. Of a close, wintry evening, the apartment is redolent of savors unnumbered and indescribable. A row of men sit perched upon the smooth-faced counter; a row of boys, and men too, sit on boxes and nail-kegs opposite the stove; whistling idlers stand and stare at the hoe and mop handles so nicely balanced overhead, possibly calculating if they would "hurt" much if they fell on their crowns; the iron stove roars, and growls, and sputters, from being frequently stirred up with sticks; little boys come in, every few minutes, and look up into the expressionless faces of the men sitting idly around, — or listen attentively, with open mouths, to what they happen to be gossiping about, — and then run uneasily out again: in the solemn pauses, the dull and heavy tickings of a wooden-wheeled Connecticut clock, perched up among the snuff-jars and preserve-pots, sound like Fate solemnly notching off Time, as it passes; now and then, one of them, with an acuter sense of hearing (or longer ears, perhaps) than the rest, lifts his head and announces that the "stage is coming;" and, like the turning over of your hand, all present get up and shake themselves out, against the arrival of the government messenger and the fetching in of the mail-bags.

It makes a pretty scene. Teniers might have added it to his portfolio. How extremely odd it strikes one, thinking of all the men in a little town grouped around a hot stove in a country store, under a full headway of gossip about the affairs of other people, and, to appearance, as much impressed with the weight of their responsibility as if the nation itself rested on their round shoulders.

—— Their wives at home, poor women! — else how would the affairs of the house get on? *They* must not go a-gadding; but the *lords*, — they may sit about in the post office till they have to come home for patches to their trousers'-seats, and not a word of complaint must be uttered against it!

—— Well, and the mail-coach rattles up. If in the winter, it is after dark a long while; but if it be summer weather, the sweet twilight is gloaming all over the town. Such delicious draughts of enjoyment as one may drink in, on the summer nights, at this particular hour, — draughts like the cool airs of spice islands, that play about one's temples and dally with his very heart!

The echoes of the driver's voice are to be heard all over the secluded street, — "Get up along! *G'lang!*" The heavy rattling of the wheels makes music against the sides of the meeting-house, and fills the town with the notes of its warning. The post-office door opens, and forth steps a boy to take the mail; and a pencil of light from the one or two tallow dips within projects itself far out into the desert of darkness.

The cluttered little office is instantly in a hubbub. Every eye is turned on the mail-bag and the Postmaster. At this particular moment, the latter is at his zenith. The by-standers watch him as he proceeds to void the responsible pouch of its precious contents. They count up every package, parcel, and newspaper that comes to the light, and appear as much pleased with what they discover as children are over the miscellaneous contents of their Christmas-stockings. They give their minds to the study of color, size, thickness, and relative importance of each article that is exposed.

Many of those nearest the counter, and those who, by reason of age or property-value, feel "privileged" in the place, venture upon taking a piece or two of mail-matter into their hands, which they proceed to "heft" and make shrewd computations about. Some of the more forward lads crowd up under the men's elbows; and you can find an odd head here, and an odd body there, and a spare leg or arm somewhere else, which, anatomically arranged, would fairly present you with the manners common to country boys in the post-office, at the hour when the mail arrives.

In good time, the contents of the bag are all assorted; that is to say, after waiting, and *waiting*. It would astonish an old Hollander himself, — what a dreadfully *slow* man the country Postmaster is; the more there is pressing upon him for dispatch, the less he is actually able to accomplish. Nothing confuses him, for he will not permit it. Still, the miscellaneous talk about the room does bother him, and he now and then looks up sharply over his spectacles, as a thorough school-master looks around his little realm of a school-room.

When, at length, the critical moment does come, he begins without the perceptible flutter of a nerve. "Mr. Atkins!" — he calls out, in a tone of appropriate solemnity. The gentleman by that name makes a half bow, as if he would say, "Excuse me for a moment, all hands!" — slips off his seat on the head of a barrel of Genessee flour standing in the darkest corner of the store, and supplicatingly holds out his hand above the counter. Or, if he cannot pierce the crowd, a file of good men and true pass over the documents to him from head-quarters, every one of whom embraces such opportunity to study the post-mark as the tallowy flare of the light affords him.

"Mr. Battles!" — again sings up the official at the desk. Everybody looks around to find Mr. Battles. He is sought after with as anxious care as the hundredth sheep that went astray. His acquaintance explore every corner and cranny, look one side and another of the stove-pipe, and finally respond — "Not here!" Then — "Mr. Cannikin!" He comes forward as far as the jam permits him, and is put in possession of his mail, much after the style of Mr. Atkins. Then — "Miss Fairmade!" At which some of the young men exchange jokes in a low voice, while a little boy — who has been on the lookout for his pretty sister near the counter — reaches out his tawny hand and makes an effective grab for it and carries it off.

So on, through the list. To those who go without a word to their own boxes and bring away their mails with a tap on the glass, this picture may seem an exaggeration; but back in the country, and altogether beyond town-reach, it will be recognized at a glance for the truth. Again and again have we heard our name called out in the ears of the town magnates, and received what mail matter was rightfully ours through the hands of we could not tell how many accommodating men and boys, mixed together in officious confusion.

—— On mooted points of law — especially constitutional law — the country Postmaster is strong beyond any one's estimate. He has the mother-wit to keep a handful of stray old Congressional Reports, bound and lettered, on the dusty shelf at his back, — as well as a more solid-looking copy of the Statutes, in imposing calf; and, with this legal stock in trade, he sets the town at defiance. Of course he is not to be contradicted on matters pertaining to the nation and its welfare, for, sustaining such close relations with the Government, how is it to be supposed that any other man *can* know some things as well as he? Even Goldsmith's school-master is no match for him, in the line of "arguing still." Not even a member of the President's Cabinet can give an opinion with more pragmatic precision, or deliver himself with greater assurance of the intentions of the august Washington authorities. He stands for the village Rajah — the Great Mogul — at the head of the political wigwam of the place. National politics take their local coloring by being passed through the rather opaque medium of his official commentary. He is sketched, in the party's mind, as the one man who keeps the keys, the seals, and the secrets. If a single man contemplates so reckless a step as party backsliding, or defection, *he* of all the rest is close behind him to make him quake in whatever clothes he happens to have on!

Thus does the Postmaster practically become the centre of town patronage and town consequence. All look up to him, as they do to the village flag-staff, from which the "stars and stripes" are in the habit of waving. If any grumble at this or at that, it makes very little difference: they are obliged to keep on even terms with him, and pocket all their dissatisfactions in silence. The women either like or dislike him, — and that very decidedly. The younger portion, however, are careful to drop no syllable that can reach the Postmaster's family, and so make infinite trouble for themselves.

When they trip across into the office, they expect a joke from him, rather slyly, about their distant correspondents, — which shows with what studious thoroughness he informs himself, and what a memory, passing all wonder, he has. Indeed, it affords him intense satisfaction to poke fun at the girls about their beaux, and to tease them with intent to draw forth still more of their little love-secrets.

Thus, no doubt, would he like to pass long afternoons, alternately running over odd papers which tardy subscribers have failed to call for, and gossiping with the girls concerning the trifling love-secrets that form the staple of their letters from places not always very far off.

It is, therefore, an unpardonable mistake to take city postmasters — the New York, and Philadelphia, and Boston magnates — as the fair representatives of these officials throughout the land. If you would make a study of the Postmaster, you must contemplate those who compose, under government favor, the rank-and-file of the office-holding army. In the rural districts the real Postmaster excels. There he stands forth, statuesque in his glory, — columnar and individual in the social landscape. The whole town leans on him, — revolves around him. He attracts all local and personal interests, like iron-filings, to his official lodestone.

THE POOR-HOUSE.

THERE is many a person who is born with a dread of some day "coming on the town;" and they actually do what they are able — unwittingly, of course — to realize their fears. Theirs is a peculiarly unfortunate inheritance; for, by all odds, the continual shrinking from imaginary evil is the cruelest test of the elasticity of the human spirit.

—— Yet we are not ourselves to forget that the author of the immortal Declaration died poor, leaving his friends to devise a friendly lottery-scheme on his behalf; and another Virginia President's remains lay for many a year without so much as a slab of stone to mark the spot where they were buried; and a wealthy patriot like Robert Morris, — the financier of the Revolution, whose Hercules shoulder lifted our national wagon out of the miry difficulties in which it was set, — even he was thrown into jail for debt, and suffered what common souls cannot conceive of.

Perhaps, too, these timid ones have some of them heard of Columbus in chains; or of Captain John Smith in a London hovel, dying in beggary and want; or of Beau Brummel coming to a pauper's end in a mendicant hospital at Caen; or they reflect that, since the periodic revulsions of these latter days have held the social road, our most affluent men are suddenly smitten as with a leprosy, and cast down into the pit of beggary and despair. There is, after all, much more in these things than either the careless or self-reliant person dreams of; and what wonder, then, that there should at least be *some* to live and die in the dark cloud of this fear, making their world hardly more than a cruel system of imprisonment.

The Poor-house is but a dismal, doleful place, at best. In many of the country towns of New England, the town's poor — nicknamed paupers — are regularly hired out to the lowest bidder. He takes the job off the town's hands, risks from sickness and death thrown in. He estimates pretty closely how much work he may be able to wring out of this one on the farm, and of that one in the house, and of a third in the shop or at the saw-mill. He prudently reckons their capacity for labor, their average stock of health, their sum total of appetite, and the proximate expense of clothing them, just as the man of the South used to reckon expenses and income for a gang of negroes he thought to purchase and put into his fields; and if it so happens, at any time in the course of the year, that the balance shows signs of going over to the wrong side of the account, is he not fruitful enough in expedients, and sharp enough, and has he not at his disposal nerve enough, too, to experiment on a reduction in fuel or fare, or at any point, in fact, where he is likely to make himself good against that horrible ogre — *a loss?*

I do actually know I should prefer to die outright, to going to the Poor-house, such as that institution commonly stands out in the social landscape. In the first place, there is no warm or tender feeling there, nothing that can begin to compensate a suffering heart for the losses it has already incurred. It is a dismal place, too. It seems to stand off at such a distance from social life, like some of the pest-houses that were set apart in the fields or woods, in other days. It bears no more relation to the word Home than the common hospital does, if indeed so much. No spirit of love sits at its cheerless hearths; no warm lights of affection, or even of hope, ever break through its dingy windows. No symptoms of elastic, healthy life are there. Only ghosts of human spirits, traversing without purpose the empty chambers and echoing halls. It is the Bastile of society, whose ponderous key, after the cruel walls shall have been thrown down, I trust will be hung above the mantel of some great humanitarian redeemer.

But, of all other things, a *country* Poor-house! — where the traffic in human flesh and human souls is just as much winked at as it ever was in the Brazils, or Cuba; where human wretches and wrecks are brought, after the world is well through with them, and made to give up still another instalment of service, for the benefit chiefly of him who gets the contract! Last year, you might have found them quartered at the farthest limit of the town, and with a proper keeper, perhaps, whose character was the best pledge of his kindness; this year, they have been huddled off, in cold and stormy weather, to the opposite town limit, — anywhere from three to seven miles distant, — and put under the iron thumb of a man who has no soul himself, nor stops to ask if others are any better endowed than he. And the next year — God help them! They no more know who their owner may be than so many Virginia slaves in a Richmond pen!

—— There appears before my eyes, this moment, the whitewashed stone structure, looking so very hard and cruel, that formed one of the social outworks of my native town, — a low, gloomy building, with a prison-like entrance into a stone-paved hall, and long benches standing against the walls outside, whereon many a weary heart has sat with its sorrowful burdens, that has since entered upon a more cheerful lot. My young imagination always associated these objects on the outside benches with lives of wretchedness, drearily dragged out to their end, — and figures of bent and wasted men and women, muttering to themselves snatches of the rosy memories which had their bloom far, far back in youth.

On the pleasant Saturday afternoons a squad of us — all "good boys," of course — were used to ramble across the river, to gratify nothing better than a morbid curiosity, or, possibly, a fugitive impulse with a dash of humor in it; — and never did my feet point themselves home again from that place, without an almost audible thanksgiving in my heart. Glad enough was I to feel that I still had a home, where all the boyish fancies and sentiments might brood. Secretly, but continually, I rejoiced that there was still a *something* between me and the poor-house. As the recollection of those decrepit figures, those wan and wrinkled faces, those profoundly sad eyes returned upon me so vividly, I quickened my pace to be farther from so dreary a scene. And still a morbid desire drew me back again; and on the very next Saturday afternoon we were all of us prowling about the dingy premises once more, watching with boyish intentness for the regular coming in and going out of our wretched favorites.

There was one thin, little, sharp-featured woman, who was reputed love-cracked; she wandered about without any sort of restraint, and without shoes, at that; and dressed in extremely short clothes. Her gray, elfin-like hair was clipped close, with the exception of a couple of horn-locks, and her high forehead was plaited with the very finest of wrinkles. She had a habit of starting up suddenly from her seat, and hurrying to touch her fingers to some particular object, — perhaps no more than a nail-head on the floor, — that momentarily attracted her. Down she sat in one of the ash-bottomed chairs, and up she got as quick as she sat down. All the while her thin lips were in motion, mumbling or whispering. Some of the other paupers insisted that she was talking of the unfaithful one who had brought her to her present wretched estate; and some declared she was in league with the Evil One, to destroy all within the house; and the rest were satisfied to treat her with a mild and inefficient sort of disdain, as if mere compassion would scarcely cover a case so peculiar. But those little gray eyes, now twinkling with fragmentary intelligence, and now glaring at you as if they would pierce you through,—those two or three elfin-locks, beaten with the rains and blanched with the winds for many a year,—that thin and slightly bent form, clad so scantily and ever in such active motion,—all these will hold fast in my memory, though I should live to reach fourscore.

Then there was an idiotic fellow in the group, who furnished us a good share of our amusement in those days. He said little, of course, and those few articulations were so indistinct and accompanied with such grimaces and facial distortions as to fairly frighten us. He never tired of asking for *a cent;*—"Do-do-*do* gi' me c-c-*cent!*" And he implored us for *a cracker* with such a hideous squint of his eye, and twist of his lower jaw, and roll of his thick tongue, as to make us laugh out even while we felt such true compassion.

Still another creature-character there was, who chanced to be gifted with just intelligence enough to feel sure that he was brighter than the idiotic subject; he was a clear "better-than-thou" individual, and so far as poor foolish *Sam* was concerned, delighted to betray it. He was a great talker, and had the eyes of a lobster, and a tongue that would crowd itself out of his mouth. If he saw that Sam was furnishing us with amusement, up he came to display his own superior parts upon so gloomy a foil. It would indeed be a pity if one *could not* shine, with a poor idiot to furnish the background. This voluble fellow took upon himself an immensely patronizing care of the other, as if, in some time past, he might have been appointed his guardian. He would come up and pull down the upraised hands of the pitiful fool, and offer him advice about what he ought to do and say before us. "Seems to me" — he would break out, with a proud glance around on us — "Sam don't know nothin' at all! He-he-he!" Then he would order him to ask for his cracker, or his cent; and suddenly turn his back upon him, and laugh, neither he nor we knew at what.

At length this very fellow came to amuse us most of all, though he little dreamed it was so. We used to *nudge* one another, and get ourselves all prepared to enjoy these displays of his fancied superiority over the weaker fool. The trick fails to provoke the same astonishment now, since the world has opened its wider view to me.

The remainder of that pauper regiment comes up before me in review, clad in their cheap and scant pauper uniform. Black and white — men and women — old and young, — alas! alas! for the pledges and promises and false lights of our social system! A decayed, unhappy, aimless race; consumed of "dry rot;" thrust out and kept out of the social world by the hand of actual benevolence; shut up from the living sympathy of their fellow-creatures; faded, worn, and broken, waiting in a sort of sullen silence for the opening of the great door that swings on golden hinges, and is to let them into a light which no man can obstruct any more.

—— A Poor-house starts strange thoughts, out of time and tune, harsh and dissonant, — which cannot instantly be put down. You find there persons whose lives had as promising a beginning as your own, but who have been able, out of the body of their combined exertions and aspirations, to reach but this inauspicious goal. There, too, you see, close beside such, other persons whose natures had foul stains on them from the beginning, which would not wash out; and whose very presence imparts to the place a lazaar-house character, as if it were actually peopled with moral infections. And pale and suffering women, too, who have vainly followed, in the blindness of love, faithless and forgetful husbands, till their wearied feet have finally brought them to this common refuge of sorrow and despair. Or, now and then, may be caught the glimpse of a child's face, little realizing how deeply the brand of Pauper is to be burned into its after life.

And always may be found there, gathered as into a mouldering corner, the relics of an once vigorous generation, mumbling the broken histories of their early life, crouching in dim and shadowy recesses, chatting of happy times such as this world will never bring them again, sitting on long benches in the sun and idly watching the flies, and, let us hope, now and then catching a glimpse of the far-off reality which they fondly believe will one day be theirs.

—— Heaven keep all of us clear of the Poorhouse! It is a place, the sight of which can check the current suddenly in young veins. Distinct and lonely it stands out in the plane of the thoughts, just as it does in the lap of the landscape. It has no other effect than to excite inward fears and bring on sudden creepings and shudderings. There is no token whatever, within it or about it, of the blessed life that lies concealed in the single word — HOME! a word that, next to Mother, lives and lingers longest in the human heart.

THE DISTRICT SCHOOL.

THAT noted polygamist and wife-murderer, known as Henry the Eighth, did no more for the cause of learning in Old England when he invited Erasmus over to take a Greek Professorship at Oxford, than our puritan ancestry, when they built the first school-house in the New England woods. Through its humble door has passed the power that is to-day engaged in conquering and civilizing the continent.

—— At the time when *I* knew it, the little red school-house stood at the fork of the road; and though there were other school-houses in other districts of the town, this was accounted the only one of which special mention was thought worthy to be made.

Mr. John Porringer — a man somewhere within the broad-growing shadows of forty-five years — "kept" this school, and was in the way of keeping it so long as he lived and liked. The notion seemed to have taken root in town, that he held a sort of life-lease of the building, if it should be used so long for the ends of education. If — here and there — one and another did rub his eyes and wonder if nobody else could keep that school as well as Mr. John Porringer, an opiate was newly administered by some mysterious process, and people soon forgot to ask the question altogether.

A seven-by-nine vestibule, constructed of rough boards, contained the pail of water, with the bright tin dipper bobbing about on the surface, — while all over its three sides pegs and nails were driven, that bore large crops of juvenile clothing, assorted and graded to the ages and sizes of its wearers. In winter you might have mistaken it for a shop, where some dealer kept sleds and skates to sell; and the junks of snow brought in on the stout boots of the boys would have charmed even a school committee all the way from Nova Zembla on runners.

In the summer time Mr. Porringer surrendered his rule and frown, and went to ploughing and hoeing and laying stone wall on the farm, thereby making an opening for somebody of secondary ability. The larger boys and girls being in demand at home during the warm months, in a general way, a quiet female teacher was thought equal to the management of the few small ones remaining; and the town paid her at the rate of two dollars per week with the privilege of "boarding herself." All this arrangement was but little better than an infant school, however, to which industrious mothers sent their weans to keep them from under foot, and give them the chance of a couple of sweet naps a day across the hard benches.

The school-room was in its blaze of glory in the winter. Then Mr. Porringer returned, to resume the magisterial badges, — the royal sceptre and crown.

—— He was a picture, and so stands out before my eyes to this day, — a tall, lank, bony person, with feet and hands of pretty similar dimensions; a head high and narrow, with a prodigious phrenological slope from the crown; stiff, straight hair, and fiercely black, brushed in a peak above the regions of his intellect; with a long, swallow-tail coat, worn shiny at elbows, cuffs, and shoulder-blades; a small, sharp eye, prowling within the thickets of overhanging eyebrows; and a pair of feet "done up" in blue woollen socks and calf-skin slippers: — these formed the several items of his scholastic motley. Yet he was accounted a wonder, in his way. Goldsmith's village school-master was out of hail entirely, with all his acquaintance with the "rules," and his unchallenged skill at "logic."

As he called out the classes to their recitations in the forenoon, he had a bustling trick of spanking a book across his palm before beginning the exercise, and sounding up in a high key — "Now, then, let 's see who 's going to be *smart* to-day!"

The large scholars were ranged around at desks that lined three sides of the room; while on the fourth was perched the sentry-box he occupied himself, in which he used to sit and rap with his ferule, or adroitly pitch heavy books at the pates of astonished offenders.

The everlasting iron stove stood out in the middle of the floor, roaring as it always roars when over-fed, and radiating wavering columns of heat till very late in the afternoons. For their own good, the children who sat about that instrument might just as well have been crowded into its own fiery bowels, as stowed in that suffocating school-room. If there chance to be any of them on the planet yet, I need not ask them if they think their early school-house baking has helped them to see their way in the world with any more clearness, or "do the sums" of life with any more readiness and rapidity.

The little fellows on the low benches nearest the stove sat as still as mice in a cupboard, and went on industriously roasting their heads and shortening their lives. Sometimes, when their faces grew as red as pearmain apples, they screened them with their spelling-books, that were carefully covered with calico; or, if they grew squirmy in the process of roasting, Mr. Porringer sternly rebuked them, declared, with a heavy stamp of his foot and in a loud voice, that there must be no *noise*, and very often caught up his ferule and shook it with a frown. Or, again, if they timidly begged to go into the entry and get a drink of water from the pail, he seemed to take a secret delight in refusing, telling them it was all nonsense for them to be drinking so much water in the winter time. Yet he permitted himself, now and then, to go to the door for a snuff of fresh air, or to enjoy a clean and cooling drink, and perhaps lay in a new quid of Virginia twist besides.

Thus and there did they bake and stew and simmer together. Boys on one side of the room, and girls on the other. Big boys and little boys, — big girls and little girls. The little boys looking up inquiringly at the big ones, to learn what might be the very newest tricks, — and little girls on their side watching the big ones, lest something worth knowing might escape them. Some conning their lessons with an intense eagerness that would make one learned in less than a winter's season. Some with books close to their faces, whispering and jabbering and working their jaws, as if they conquered their tasks by the process of mastication. Little boys slyly sticking pins through their neighbors' trousers, or pulling their flaxen hair where it *would* go straying, or chewing cuds of paper and snapping them spat against the ceiling, to make the girls laugh.

Above the din rose the voice of Mr. Porringer, — "Next! parse *Might have loved*, and see if you can't put it in the right mood and tense!" — a matter very difficult of performance even by learners much older than any who sat on those benches. A droning hum rising in the ears from all quarters of the room, like the dry heat simmering up from the stove in the middle of the floor. A shifting scene of faces, — some older and some younger, some scowling and some smiling, — some studying the lessons and some studying mischief, — yet every one intent on getting through at the easiest rate.

And, to vary the picture ever so little, a broad-shouldered negro fellow sitting all by himself in the corner next the door, his ebony countenance fairly sweating fun and mischief at every pore. He was the "black top" of the little school parish, — the fifth wheel of the educational coach. Over the top of his slate his twinkling little eyes took sly observations, from time to time, of what was going on about the room, and he laughed under his breath at any trifling trick he saw played, though sometimes he could not help giving a rip of laughter that drew the eyes of the whole school round to him in an instant. Then he would begin innocently to spit on his slate and rub out his "sum," no doubt believing it rather an odd problem even in *mixed* mathematics.

He had a queer way of lifting his entire scalp when he chose to elevate his eyebrows, which set his frizzled pelt in such comical motion that none of us could possibly resist it. Mr. Porringer's ruler was brandished at the little fellows pretty often, on these occasions, but we could not help wondering how it was he never seemed to see our African exemplar. It so happened, too, — as it very often does happen in such cases, — that this same negro was as *clever* a creature as any human being on foot, and would positively have done himself wanton harm as soon as anybody else; yet his shining skin being always as full of drollery as a fruit-rind is of juice, it was to be expected that it would sometimes overrun for others' innocent merriment. A wonderful fellow he among the boys, grown man though *he* was; and although he worked out on a farm in the summer, he always found time to go fishing with them on the rainy days, and would gladly be off all night, wading the low streams with birch-bark torches in quest of suckers and dace.

Committee Day was the Red Letter day of the Winter's calendar. The school presented itself then, for drill and review, to the eyes and. ears of the Minister, the Deacon, and some one or two more of the local magnates, whose duty it was to make the regular inquisition of school-affairs, in the name and behalf of the town.

Mr. Porringer used to set on foot great preparations for this event of the year, scouring up the little knowledge of his pupils till they scarcely recognized themselves in their transformation. None of us could have been more nervous over our expectations than he was for himself; and yet, the Committee out of the account, nobody could be more positive and despotically dogmatic about his knowledge than this same Mr. John Porringer.

When this dignified body of (usually) three men entered, looking, as somebody ventures it, as "wise as saws and modern instances," if not a trifle more so than that even, the Master met them at the door; not blandly, as a June morning gets in among the cherry-blossoms, but stiffly, and with an empty dignity that originated with nothing and amounted to nothing. Bowing, with one hand outstretched, towards the Committee, he lifted the other, which held his book, as a signal for the school to rise in respect; and the seating of that body again made as great confusion as the fainting of a lady at College Commencement.

The classes were then called up, — all the way from the A, B, abs to the students in Arithmetic and Geography. The small fry were ordered to toe a crack running the length of the oak floor, and in that position to make their "manners." It was so seriously done, that I cannot keep back the laugh, even now, in recalling it. Some of the answers to questions were given by the larger classes in a yell of unison, loud enough to scare every stray bear from the back settlements. Then, more hickory in the stove — more roasting of young heads — and more internal applications of cold water from the dipper in the entry.

Finally, the recitations over, there followed a demand from Mr. Porringer for "silence!" and a second demand upon the Committee for "any remarks," &c. The homilies there spoken, I well remember, were German-text to us all; we knew nothing what they meant, and cared nothing whatever for them. At the end, a prayer from the Minister, — a general rising of the school, — more bowing, — and a welcome *exit* through the outer door.

And so the review was over.

Mr. Porringer would seal up the entire parcel with some little speech of his own, and thus it remained until visitation day came round again the next winter. We were then let out, the padlock was fastened in the staple of the door, the fire in the stove went down, and we saw no more of Mr. Porringer till fully nine o'clock the next morning.

COCK-CROW.

Cock-a-doodle-do!
Where away is the morn,
That you sound your clarion-horn?
Not a streak of light in the east,
Nor the faintest ray
Of dappled gray
Is yet to be seen, — not the least.
Three o'clock! — that is all;
And still you sound your call
To all within the house to wake,
And into their hearts their burdens take,
Before ever the day is born!
There is not a sign of the dawn;
The stars are burning out, 't is true,
But no eyes see the day yet coming through;
The world is fast asleep in the dark;
Not so much as the sound of the watch-
dog's bark;
And still this Cock-a-doodle-do!

Cock-a-doodle-*do!*
The first rich ray of red

Has fallen across the shed:
And, from his perch, once more the call
Of the warder that keeps watch for us all.
Shrill, and clear, and high is the note
From out that regal throat,
Pulsing its echoes everywhere
Through the frosty morning air,
Down the valley clear to the mill,
And away to the top of the nearest hill.
The cattle get up from their long night's bed,
And the boards of the floor creak overhead;
The horse looks out from his darkened stall,
Like a lord from the door of his castle-hall;
Over the roof curls up the smoke
That tells of the stir of thrifty folk;
The hens on their perches crowd along,
Aroused by their lord's resounding song.
And now the sun's clear, golden ray
Falls through the barn-chinks on the hay;
Into the pails full many a stream
Of milk, that is rich with clotted cream,
Riddles the foam in a zigzag line,
As sweet as the breath of the yarded kine.

Cock-a-doodle-*do!*
There he is, on the garden gate,
Crest erect, and spirit elate;
The rain has been falling all the day
And no eye now can thread its way
To any rift or lift in the clouds

That pack the concave in such crowds:—
But chanticleer, he sees the sign,
Where wisest men can read no line;
A prophet, with an instinct high,
He keeps the secret of the sky,—
A favorite child of Nature he,
That knows the heart of her mystery.
And at that Cock-a-doodle-do,
And cheery flap of pinions, too,
The household to the windows go,
In answer to the call they know:—
The sky grows brighter, and the blue
Comes forth at Cock-a-doodle-do!

Cock-a-doodle-*do!*
The rival he has overthrown
Goes reeling to his roost alone;
And he, the royal conqueror,
With bloody ruff about his throat,
Sends forth his strong, defiant note
To Chanticleers near and remote,
On every farmer's broad barn-floor.
No shouts from the walls of proud old Troy
Were ever given with half the joy
That fills the heart of this brave bird,
As he makes the news of his victory heard.
You 'd think he was some baron bold,
From whom the rest their tenures hold,
Proclaiming, on the garden wall,
His feudal watch and ward for all.

Cock-a-doodle-*do!*
No house is Home, without that horn
To sound the hours, from dawn to dawn.
Before the eye rise curling smokes,
That come from fires of country folks, —
A stack of roofs, — a low, wide door, —
The thump of flails on a big barn-floor, —
A tented field of corn hard by,
About whose stacks great pumpkins lie, —
Hens' nests snug hidden in the hay,
And children hunting half the day, —
A garden filled with fruits and flowers,
Where birds make musical the hours, —
Good cheer, warm welcomes, and bright fires,
That fill the wishing heart's desires.
Oh, Chanticleer! — brave Chanticleer!
Thy voice rings through all History;
Outstarting from the mystery
Of Indian jungles, dark and drear,
Thy path has lain through Greece and Rome
To the door of every farmer's home;
They stamped thee on their ancient coins,
And offered thee in sacrifice
Unto their heathen deities,
That sprung from mythologic loins:
And "Plato's man" thou wert, we know,
Above two thousand years ago;
And Peter felt his shameful lie
Reproved by thy shrill, chiding cry,
And went out, weeping bitterly.

Thy note sends every ghost to bed,
Afraid to show its guilty head
When the shadows of the night have sped.
They set thee on the tallest spires,
Above the fog of earth's desires,
A sort of lookout in the sky,
Interpreter of wet and dry,
And cheering souls to victory.

Thy Cock-a-doodle-do, it rings
Through Winters, Autumns, Summers, Springs;
At every hearth, in every heart,
The tenderest feelings take a start:
Thou mayst not be the bird of Jove,—
Thou art a bird that all men love:
There is no fowl that walks, the peer
Of strutting, crowing Chanticleer!

BOOK THIRD.

BUCOLICS.

" Let me be no assistant for a State,
But keep a Farm and Carters."
SHAKSPEARE — " HAMLET."

A DAY'S WORK ON THE FARM.

A WELL-ORDERED farm is a little republic, having its President and its Ministers of State. Every day brings its duties, recurring with the rising and setting of the sun. Matters do not go on by a bell, as in a rattling factory town; but they come round in as unbroken an order, describing as perfect a circle, and representing as momentous interests.

—— At three o'olock in the morning, Cock-crow. The feathered lord's perch is in the basement of the barn, and his clarion sounds muffled and distant. A second, awaiting but this well-known signal from his elder, erects himself proudly beside his dames and sounds a lustier note, with a strain of defiance in it. Then a third, and a fourth; and presently every cock that has sway over a harem in the country neighborhood sends forth his shrill token of the coming of the morn. They call, one to the other, from farm to farm, and from hill-side to valley. The still air suddenly becomes alive. Every barn-yard gives cheery welcome to the breaking day. The households, far and wide, awake, and know that the gates of the day are soon to be opened wide.

The farmer who pretends to be a farmer indeed, dresses and calls his help; while the housewife is pottering over pans and kettles in the kitchen, making ready to roast and fry, stew and bake, in the big fireplace where so many rows of pot-hooks hang from the crane. The men trudge off, half awake, to the cow-yard, and the milk is soon churning into the foaming pails between their knees. About the door troop old hens with chickens in charge, clucking and scratching as busily as if the whole summer-day were not before them, and no bugs and flies out of bed, either. The cat goes purring around the kitchen and the door-step, rubbing herself affectionately against one and another, and tendering expressions of her joy at seeing the family about once more.

When the hired men and boys have soused their heads in the freshly drawn water that stands on the bench outside, and the milking is done, they go to the sheds and barns and out-buildings to get ready the tools with which their day's work is to be accomplished.

Whether it be over carts and chains and harrows and ploughs, or scythes and cradles and rakes and wagons, the yard is, for some little time, a scene of life and bustling activity.

All this while, too, preparations are making in the house for breakfast; and when it is finally announced, and the feet of hungry men have been scraped at the door, the work at the board suggests nothing so much as the work in the fields afterwards. The eating is not minced, if the meat is. Every dish has a relish of its own. A piece of cold meat is a piece of cold meat, to be eaten without misgivings of dyspepsia and indigestion. Simple as the table is, it is loaded with the fat of the land. Who that knows new milk and fresh cream, yellow butter or new-laid eggs, but takes in the picture with a single recollection?

If it be Spring-time, — when buds are bursting, and leaves expanding to the sun, and steamy smokes are working up from valley and hill-side, and calves are bleating from the yard for mothers that call them from the pastures, and life sparkles again in the running brooks, and waters glisten in little pools all about the lowlands, — the man of the hard hands, but soft heart, is turning up the sod with the gleaming share, his boy astride the old plough-horse, while he "gees" and "haws" the yoke of cattle himself; or, in other fields, sowing his grain with the hand of faith, and walking his acres in the spirit of a lord.

Then the bustle is in the barns, the sheds, the corn-cribs, and the cellars, where they sort their seeds, prepare the corn with plaster for planting, and slice baskets of potatoes, for burial in the hills. Horses are hitched into this and into that; cattle straggle over the yard, rattling their yoke-rings; wagons are rolled out, and others dragged in; the turkeys are stealing off to find places for nests; and hens are cackling over the egg apiece they have hidden away with such pains on the barn scaffolds. Withal, the sun glows warm and cheerful, and the heart expands and becomes more genial in the influence of its penetrating heat.

All day long they plough and harrow and drop seeds, and cover with the hoe. The boys are very tired before night falls, and come pretty near falling asleep while they wash their feet out the door at evening. Little enough money goes toward candles after supper, for all hands are glad enough to go off to bed pretty soon after their day's work is over. And the whole house shortly becomes silent again, — the silver moon, perhaps, throwing over its spreading roof a silent blessing.

—— Or, in the Autumn, the days are just as full of activity and life. Harvesting has somewhat of sentiment in it. A man cannot walk among the spires of his rustling corn, or pile the yellow pumpkins in his creaking wain, or stand out solitary and alone in the glorious landscape, looking dreamily on the bewildering colors of distant woods and forests, without feeling his heart fill, and at times even his eyes overflow.

The corn goes into the cribs, slender and golden. The apples are rolled away in barrels, or emptied into bins for early using. The potatoes are digged and carried off to the cellars. Stalks are stacked in spare places about the barns and sheds, and the bouncing pumpkins are rolled all over the barn-floor. Then every space is filled; the harvest has been abundant, and the granaries are ready to burst with the superfluity. The cattle begin to come in from the pastures, and stand grouped near the bars, idly butting one another with their horns.

There is no telling how long the fine weather is to last, nor how soon the dull fall rains and blustering snows may be upon them; therefore the farmer holds steadily to his work from morning till night, — going and coming, filling and emptying continually. Now he can see the delightful fruits of his summer's labor. He finds that his returns are enriching him, and that poverty and want are exiled from *his* hearth, at least during the coming winter.

—— In the haying season, which every one knows to be the hardest of the year, the women clear the breakfast-table as soon as the meal is over, wash up the dishes, and hurry to finish their tasks at the churn or cheese-tub. Or, taking time by the forelock, they go about getting dinner, — no sentimental task, where there are from six to a dozen hungry haymakers to be fed. So into the garden they go for the vegetables, — cabbages, peas, beets, early beans, and whatever else offers to their dextrous hands. Having digged the potatoes, the boys are off in the field with the mowers.

By-and-by, pots are boiling, and the fire is crackling; the kitchen is as hot as roast, and the good wife's face glows with the burnish of a ripe tomato. The daughters are at the sink, or going here and there to save steps for their mother. By the middle of the forenoon, the boys come in to carry luncheon to the haymakers, packed in a great market-basket, —

bread-and-butter, cheese, cold meats, and apple pies. In a pail, or a stone pitcher, is the sweetened water, black with syruppy richness, and flecked all over its surface with little floating islands of ginger.

They all go off together, in the morning, down the road, or the lane, till they come to the bars through which they are to turn in. It is not long before they have swung their scythes and taken their positions; and you can catch the hoarse ring of their blades as they go rasping and cutting through the waist-high grass. It is done as by magic. The face of the whole field is changed in a few hours. The grass lies heavy and wet in the swathes, and men and boys are spreading it, with pitchforks and rake-handles, in the scorching sun. At intervals you can hear the noise of the rifling of the scythes, sounding in the distance like a strain of music in the airs of the July morning; musical, because so in harmony with the scene and the season.

The morning being well spent, the workers withdraw beneath some spreading tree, — a maple, or a young hickory, or, perchance, an ancient meadow elm, — and there on the clean, sweet grass eat and drink their forenoon fill, not unmindful of the coming dinner and the nooning spell. The basket is well rummaged and lightened ; the stone pitcher passes from hand to hand, every long draught lowering the sweet tide till little is left but the ridges of ginger that have been stranded on its throat and sides. A few jokes — a little laughter — a passage of half-play with the boys as they stretch themselves on the grass, — and work is resumed again.

From that time until the dinner-horn sounds, no tented field, whether of tourney or military encampment, ever furnished a busier or more picturesque spectacle. The sun flames high overhead, pouring down almost perpendicularly its fervid streams. Lines of heat dance and waver as far as the eye can reach across the slopes and plain, and seem to open wider the million pores as you regard their dizzy motion.

When the horn blows, the men stack their implements of husbandry in the nearest shade, and go home in the wagons, or straggling back up the lane, a wearier phalanx than when they came forth in the dewy morning. They have done much work in those few hours, and done it well.

The "women-folks" have got through their steaming forenoon labors over the dinner, and now stand ready to wait on the hearty fellows who are returned to test the bounty and quality of their culinary skill. Having drawn up to the board, the laborers find the meats already carved, and fall to with a relish such as no dainty appetite ever found in the bottom of a bitters-bottle.

All sorts of vegetables, smoking hot; pork, in solid fat cuts, right out of the deep soundings of the barrel; beef, red and ripe, and richly streaked with fat from end to end; white bread and brown, in piles like barricades; and puddings or pies, as it may chance, — together with such other garnish as is to be found in true state on no tables but those of the lords of the land. The whole board is a parterre of steams, and smokes, and fragrance! The appetizing fumes of meat and vegetables steal through doors and windows, and persist in finding their way even into the "best room" of all in the house.

These rugged, robust mowers eat very much as they go about their other work; and as soon as they have swallowed their last mouthful, and washed their throats with the last draught of cold water, they push back noisily in their chairs, wipe their mouths with their sleeves, and catch a long breath, as of regret, to recover.

The table has been cleared as by some process of magic. The pies — they have been whittled in pieces. The board is but a wreck of fragments, — *disjecta membra* of the noonday feast, — which they turn their backs upon as soon as they have been surfeited, going out to sit upon the logs before the door, or to lie down for a little upon the sun-checkered grass.

By afternoon, the hay requires turning; oftener before. In the latter case, it is raked into windrows pretty soon after dinner, and got ready either to be cocked or carried in, load by load.

When the pitching, and loading, and "raking after" is ready to be done, the field presents a sight even more full of life than during the morning. This they all consider — the boys in particular — the very jolliest part of the day; for now the hands are close enough in company to tell their old country stories over again, and pass about their smoky jokes. And, by the help of such stimulus, the big, round loads of sweet hay go off out of the field, one by one, and all are carefully "mowed away" for winter's use beneath the broad barn roof.

With still another wash and thorough face-scrubbing at the bench without the back door, they all pass in to supper. It is ready for them at sundown, and has cost but little time in its preparation. The women have been sewing and chatting through the afternoon, sitting in a clean, cool room, and quite as busy at their work as were the "men folks" at theirs.

Though the supper is frugal and plain, it is ample and good. They come to it with a relish. Meat for the third — fourth time during the day. Such as prefer milk may dip it from a large pan for themselves, and eat the crumbled and sopped bread out of it till they are full. After supper, the milking of the cows, already yarded; then a short stroll about the premises through the hushed twilight hour; and finally, tired and fagged, to welcome beds under the roof. If any men do indeed enjoy sleep, they are the haymakers. It comes sweet and undisturbed to their heavy lids, with no nightmares to make sounding rapids in its placid current.

—— A day's work on a farm, at any season in the year, is no "gentleman's" work at all, but the hardest that can be done. Mechanical inventions are, to be sure, doing much to relieve the husbandman; yet no such go-betweens can remove the care, and anxiety, and personal labor of it all; and no man knows of what he talks, when he thinks to go about farming as he would go off to fish, — lazily, and brimming over with sentiment and dreams.

FARMERS' WIVES.

IN this country, the wife of the farmer stands at the head of society. She may not know it, yet it is gospel truth. Beginning back with the foundation, or elements, of our social system, we find that she is at the bottom of all the bold and brave enterprises that have made us great, and has sustained the burden and heat of the whole day in our national growth and advancement. And it is because she has had the making of *the men*, training and moulding them from the very gristle of boyhood.

She has carried the entire fabric in her heart; since upon her have our heroes relied, and to her looked for the sweetest approbation. The wives of the farmers were the real Women of the Revolution, of whom never can too much be said in praise. Little or nothing could have been done without their aid.

The wife, in the country, is the one being who can make the homestead beautiful. She calls into it the atmosphere of genuine love. She is the single and powerful magnet, by which husband and children are attracted there. She can make all things bright and lovely, — or she can bring down cloudiness and gloom, put everybody in the sulks, and set the whole household to wishing they were established somewhere else.

A woman can do *as much* as that, with great ease, anywhere; but in a home in the country, she has full and peculiar power. It is not so easy to get away from a home in the seclusion of rustic life, that is notoriously uncomfortable; but in the changing crowd of a large city, it is a very different matter.

Farmers' wives are scarcely aware of their influence; if they were, they might at times employ it to better immediate purpose. They practically underrate themselves, to begin with. They run to one extreme, and consider themselves of no consequence in the world at all; and then they run to the other, and insist that they are just as good as anybody else. Which, of course, they are. A little brush — the least in the world — of city influence, and they are all in a flutter; instantly they are ready to forget the beauty and the endearing associations of their country home-life, and to make themselves unhappy with envy of their city cousins' flounces and fanfaronade. The calm, contemplative, truly religious existence they enjoy in the heart of Nature, they undervalue at all points, and are ready to exchange it for the daily view of stony streets, the daily sounds of rattling vehicles, and the almost positive certainty of never again seeing the sun either rise or set.

—— But there is a reason for much of this unsettled feeling of hers. In the country, woman is made too much a mere *drudge.* It may sound all very romantic and sweet to your ears, dear madam, to hear the talk of the Arcadian life such a sister must lead, away from large towns and their frivolous influences, — but it is not such a life as you allow your imagination to dish up before you. Think what it is for a woman — a wife — to milk cows, to suckle calves, and sometimes to feed the pigs; to attend regularly on the ducks and chickens, besides performing various other chores not altogether in harmony with her feminine nature. Then, again, the same tasks — always hard — follow one another in a continuous round from morning till night, one day upon another; and she must be different from the rest of her sex, who can help offering silent thanksgiving when God draws the curtain of night for the world to lay its head on its pillow and go to sleep.

The English country ladies — we have all heard about them; about their fresh robustness, their rosy health, and their overflow of animal spirits. We wish one half as good news could be told of the country ladies of America, with their anxious, care-worn countenances, as if all the interests of the farm devolved — as they often do — upon themselves. In a good many cases they are a deal "smarter" than the men, and take the management out of their hands. They can reckon you up the cost and value of a hog, or a "critter," without even going near the slate that hangs inside the pantry; whereas their husbands would be studying, like industrious Champollions, all the sundry chalk-marks about the house and shed, in hopes of getting at what they wanted. If many of our farmers are asked by a travelling drover what they will take for such or such a "beef critter," they will show in a moment their disinclination (if not their inability) to sell, without first consulting "*mother*."

In this, among other ways, the woman in the country becomes gradually unfeminine, —

loses a certain degree of that bloomy freshness which so charmingly sets off female character, — mixes in with the roughness, and hardness, and drudgery, and even the dirt of farm-work and farm-life, and, in the lapse of time, unconsciously parts with some of those attractive qualities which should be found as elements in the character of every lovable female.

But to describe, rather than venture on the essayist's ground: — Most farmers' wives are up last at night and earliest in the morning. And although it is no decent man, fit to call himself an American farmer, who would let his wife rise first and make the fires of a winter's morning, yet she is both ambitious and thrifty enough to be in the kitchen very soon after he is, — bustling about the sink, the pots, the kettles, and the table, making the usual breakfast preparations, and arranging generally for the progress of the day's work. You never catch *her* idle. She moves twice as quick as her husband, and accomplishes twice as much in the same time.

Breakfast over, the day's operations begin. Every day is much like every other day in the same season. The milk is to be scalded; butter is to be churned; dishes are to be washed, and pots and kettles, tables and trays to be scoured; in the season, the young chicks are to be looked after; the children must have their faces washed, and be sent to school; luncheon must not be forgotten for the workmen in the field; dinner must be hurried into the pot or oven; the table is to be set again; then it is to be cleared off; then the sewing must be done; or company rides up to the door; and the little chicks come in once more for their share of daily attention; and the children hurry home from school, as hungry as young bear cubs; and the table must be set for tea; and the cows must be milked as soon as they come up to the yard; and the business of the day must be freely talked over with husband, as well as the plans for the morrow; and the little ones are to be got off to bed; — and then night comes down for good again upon the whole household.

This is the quintessence of routine. Little or nothing interposes to break its dull monotony. Unless the interior resources are rich and ample, the life lapses, in spite of one's self, into formal, ancient, and plodding practices, and rarely does a living jet of fresh experience enter in.

In winter-time it seems harder for the goodwife still, for then the days are — oh! so long;

shortest of all though we know them to be at the coming of the winter solstice. The monotony for the spirits is like the stretching fields of snow to the eyes, — reaching afar in the bleak distance, without a sign of boundary or neighborhood. Well might the wives of farmers keep long sticks hanging in their chimney-corners on which to notch off these weary days with their pale sunshine, as they slowly pass.

The wintry mornings dawn late, with nipping airs, and often with leaden clouds lying in long bars just above the horizon. The windows are covered with all sorts of devices in frost-work, and breaths blow out from all mouths in volumes of steam. If a fresh snow has fallen during the night, the whole world looks so still, so thoroughly hushed, and so completely buried up, that the snapping and crackling of the kindlings on the logs scarcely breaks the solemn silence of the time. Then, whether fingers ache with the cold or not, breakfast is to be made ready for the household, — often with but a single pair of hands at that. The girls should be up, and they can be of some help; but I do not incline to believe they *are* always up; — their huge, puffy feather-beds are thoroughly warmed, and the rosy creatures do hate awfully to climb out of them early in the morning, on the icy cold floor. Now and then the boys take a hand at chopping the minced meat, or help peel the smoking-hot potatoes, with long checked aprons tied close under their chins.

It is eight o'clock — nine o'clock — and even ten o'clock, sometimes, before the family work is fairly set in motion; and then, when steams float all around the blackened ceiling of the kitchen, and the savors of stewing pumpkins rise from the hardly covered mouth of the great kettle, — perhaps there are sausages to fill, or pork to pack away in the barrel, or cheeses to finish making, or butter to churn, or some other such labors to be attended to, any one of which is sufficient to tax the energies of a heroic and industrious woman.

The "men folks" may be off at work in the woods, dragging logs and chopping; but they realize little of the multiplying cares and perplexities that are sown, thick as thistle-seed, around the steps of the farmer's wife, every day. Indeed, it is a great deal more true than one generally thinks, that if a farmer, capable and thrifty himself, gets a slovenly, behindhand, incompetent helpmeet, nothing under the stars will save his farm from slowly cankering away under the application of mortgages. It is the wife who is the farmer's real support, after all. She either makes or unmakes. It is nothing to the point that he manages to drive good bargains with cattle, horses, muttons, and field products, unless she who sits at home, and weaves the web of his fortunes for him, seconds with earnestness and industry all his plans and purposes: — he does but draw water for himself in sieves, instead of buckets.

Thus the farmer's wife stands first in importance in our agricultural matters; and everybody knows full well that agriculture is the only base and bottom of civilized society.

Then, in the family group, she shapes, colors, and directs everything. The youthful character is in her hands altogether. Whether by an assumed or a conceded authority, she is the head and front of the family. She is the *heart* of the household, if she is not the *head* as well. She not only bakes and brews, but she trains boys and girls in those simple, temperate, and oftentimes Spartan habits, which subsequently project themselves with the force of a new individuality upon the destinies of the outside world.

This is the province of the farmer's wife, — no more, and no less. It does not fall to her lot to do nothing but make butter and cheese, knit stockings and spin wool, away off in the country solitudes; but she is scattering about her, every day of her life, the seeds of a grain whose products are not for a day, but for all time. If only she saw it so for herself, what a change it would work in her tasks and her lot! How fresh her resolution would become,— how perpetually revived and renewed her purposes! Instead of bewailing her hard fortune, off in such monotonous and dismal retirements, she would rather seem, in her own eyes, to sit like a queen at the heart of Nature, silently guiding and fashioning the forces that are certain, in good time, to control the whole social system.

——"Drudgery! everlasting drudgery!"— so the country wives exclaim continually. Nor can it exactly be wondered at, either. Still, there *is* something beside drudgery in it, to one who knows how and is determined to ennoble herself, and exalt her occupation. Life, we agree, is chiefly made up of little things; but even these may be lifted up by the soul of love, and made glorious.

But the husband and head is as much at fault as anybody else. He insists, dogmatically; he exacts; he lays on the heavy burdens; he sometimes even tyrannizes;— he is the single dead weight upon the frail shoulders of the woman. It is not to be gainsayed or explained away, — he shuffles off too much of the coarse labor upon her, consenting to make her the packhorse of the family establishment, the real beast of burden in all his domestic and farming plans. Out of it come, of course, low spirits, an overworked constitution, total indifference to the high ends and aims of life, and a gradual and almost entire loss of the true spiritual faculty.

—— Such should be the case no longer. The wife should stand, everywhere, for what is pure and sweet, for what is innocent and holy; not one whit less so in country than in town; nay, even *more so* in those delightful rural retreats, and amid those untainted influences which God sends, like delicious fragrance, to keep sweet the atmosphere wherein the human soul is obliged for a time to dwell.

Especially is it idle to speak in disparagement of the farmer's wife. Her city sister can display her silks, her carriage, and her list of "friends;" but what are they all, in the light of that sincere simplicity, that serene beauty of life, in which the country wife is privileged to dwell and rejoice all her days?

FARMERS' DAUGHTERS.

GOD bless them, every one!

It is an involuntary exclamation, — but what of that? Is it not, therefore, the sincerer speech of the heart?

The rosy creatures, buxom and clear of complexion, — their souls in their eyes and their hearts in their hands, — robust and bouncing, — vigorous and hearty — overflowing with life, and health, and genuine beauty! You, my pretty town cousin, may pout "*coarse!*" about them; but that is only a conventional word; it does n't mean the same thing in any two places. But there are some few things about them which we do like; — they are simple, and timid, and thoroughly *natural.* Better, a thousand times, for the hopes of the world, that the mothers of the coming generations be awkward with their stores of health, than so very fine, sentimental, and dawdling. The boys and girls who have not yet opened their bright eyes on the day, will live to give thanks to the country girls of the present generation for their priceless inheritance of physical robustness and activity. The gigantic projects of the coming years will owe their final success to the stout constitutions and high spirits which the maidens of our day are capable of transmitting.

You can find them back from the towns and cities to-day; on solitary cross-roads; in low-roofed houses, a mile or more apart; on large farms, superintending the dairy, the kitchen, or the poultry department; girls not put out to a term of hard service exactly, nor yet *kept in* for a similar purpose; but quietly and happily attending to domestic duties in a domestic way; contented, in that contentment furnishes bliss of the serenest sort; trustful with their affections; disposed to look on the bright side of things; full of song to overflowing, from morning till night; with red cheeks in summer and winter alike; attached, with a sort of devotion, to home and all its endearing associations; and, all things considered, the brightest beauties that illuminate the pathway of parents and the neighborhood.

Such are our farmers' daughters, — the best of them. They are not all, or altogether, after this picture; yet the exceptions are by no means to be found so much fault with. Those samples which we have made rapid studies of,—as you can find them all through our Northern States, and New England especially,—are really models of their sex. Perhaps a trifle too timid; perhaps not quite at ease in all kinds of society; perhaps unaware, too, of the fresh and innocent beauty that breathes and speaks from face and form;—*still*, as the town is driven to make regular drafts on the country for its men, so is it obliged, and so will it always be obliged, to go back through the same green lanes, and over the same grassy fields, and into the same brown houses, for its mothers for the generations that are yet to come. We cannot rejoice too much that it is so.

——But it ought to be stated that a farmer's girl in these days is not what a farmer's girl used to be. Once, she was tied down to paring apples and slicing them for the string, to spinning flax and wool, to indiscriminate scullery labors, and to work which is now thought not in all cases the very easiest or best for her. Now, the spinning is not performed in the farmer's kitchen, the apples are pared and cored by machinery, the hard work is carried off by the hired "help," and a general spirit of refinement is slowly working its way in. One readily detects it in the changed look of the door-yards. It smiles forth a confession in the gay masses of flowers that are tended with such care during the warm season. It betrays itself in the disposition to read more, to be less timid and shy, to establish something like a truly social state and neighborhood, and to court those graces which, always and everywhere, imply a generous culture on the part of those who give them attention.

—— And, just in this place, it is impossible to keep out of mind the influence which one graceful, beautiful, and pure-minded woman exerts in a home in the country. There *could be* no home, without her presence. No desert land could be more utterly desolate. She throws around the dwelling whatever silent, but eloquent, charms belong to her individual character. From her person itself radiates an atmosphere that seems to make of all things a heaven. By her look, — by her smile alone, she is able to light up any spot, and diffuse cheerfulness where man, by himself, would be but a melancholy hermit. Where she lives, roses blow in the earliest summer, and greenest grass creeps to the very door. The buttercups and dandelions inframe her dwelling with a border of gold, as if the very earth at her feet were a mine of yellow wealth for her. Children's footsteps patter where she goes, and merry voices are to be heard on every hand. Life accompanies her, surrounds her, and follows in her train. Beauty walks in her path. Happiness hovers about her presence, and there is hope, and rest, and peace only where she is.

—— A thriving farmer of these times is ambitious to give his daughters all the advantages he can secure for them; so he consults friends and the passing catalogues, and resolves on sending them to as good schools as are to be found for the hunting. But every mother's daughter of them knows how to make and bake bread, before she goes. And as soon as their term of "schooling" is over, and they have taken a little time to recruit their strength by a reasonable respite at the old homestead, they are competent to take charge of all the incipient households to which they are, generally, soon after called.

But not all have the luck — good or bad — to go away to school. What they get, by way of "education," they get near home, in their own district, and then set up for teachers themselves, during the summer months, under the auspices of very dignified School Committees. They go through the sing-song routine of teaching little ones how to read and spell, — perhaps they instruct the girls in plain sewing likewise, — and afterwards subside into the occupation of active assistants in their own respective households.

Sometimes they are indispensable at home; in which case they are held fast by the button of affection, and by sundry other inducements of their parents. Very soon they are installed mistresses in their own native homes, and maintain their position in spite of even the most determined efforts of admirers to entice them away. Very many such we used to know, who, with sacred devotion to mother and father, have consented to forego all their ambition, — world-wise, — and consecrated their lives to the comfort and stay of the hearts of their parents. Beautiful pictures of the true filial duty! Yet such examples are not so many as to be found without some industrious looking.

We wish, from our hearts, that all the farmers' girls could have the advantages they so much desire, and equally deserve. Some of them are mere stay-at-homes in the quiet old brown houses, and look out over the green grass, or the white snow-drifts, longing and longing to see somewhat of that great world — so restless, too! — which lies beyond. They are true to their daily engagements in the kitchen; they wash, and iron, and help in the dairy, and sew; they make beds, wash floors, set things to rights, run to the windows whenever strangers travel the road, and make up — first and last — the life and light of the household. When you take your brief summer excursion into the country, you will see them standing in the doors, or feeding the poultry in the back-yard, perchance hanging out the washing on the line, with sprawling sun-bonnets on — rosy, robust, and charming. Their faces confess health, and their forms faultlessness.

Just under the hill-side yonder, now, there are three young girls beneath the shelter of the same roof. The farmer himself will give you warm welcome, and, with a knowing and humorous nod, tell you that the woman across the supper-table, with the long apron on, is his wife. Then walk in Jane, and Lucy, and Betsey; you see they stick to the old-fashioned names. They drop a timid courtesy, fall to fussing over their collars and wristbands, and run about the room to make you — and themselves, too — more comfortable.

Or, if it happens to be before supper, and

perhaps a winter's evening too, you sit waiting in the chimney-corner, until the table is spread and ready. In that interval, you have a fine chance to see how the domestic arrangements work. You get an inkling of the family discipline, and find out on the spot what farmers' daughters are good for. Jane "draws" the tea; Lucy hunts out the mince-pies, slices the bread, keeps the cat from mischief about the hearth, and has a corner of her twinkling eye for the new guest; while Betsey takes care of the younger children, watches to see that the bread does not burn before the fire, runs here and there as her mother calls, and keeps an eye on the stranger, as well as her sister. And these three buxom rustic Graces form a truly beautiful household picture. Father sits back in his corner chair, regarding the girls with secret delight; and mother bustles about, not forgetting to throw an occasional eye to the stranger herself.

The girls are up betimes in the morning, with a window wide open and a bed soon made; and in the summer mornings you will see them everywhere around and within the house. Sometimes up at the barn-yard milk ing a favorite cow, — or throwing corn to the ducks, geese, and turkeys, — or stuffing dough down the gaping throats of downy chickens. They are gay creatures then, — romping hoydens, with cheeks like June roses, and arms bared to sun and air. It would be no such hard work to fall straight in love with them.

If cheese is making, they have hands to dip into the crumbling curd; or if butter, their fair arms are kneading out the buttermilk from the golden mass as deeply as they can thrust them in. Of good, substantial housekeeping, they know just all that is worth knowing, from starting a fire in a frosty morning to basting a goose and bringing it in proper trim to table. None are more thoroughly "up" to all the essential tricks of living. Even when they pour the milk from the pitcher, as you sit over against them at the table, it looks and sounds as it does not anywhere else; your lips instinctively water for a tumbler-full before it is set down again; and ever after, when you think of fresh country milk and cream, it is along with country maids, fair arms, and ruddy faces.

It is at the Singing School where our buxom country girl finds her future husband. Nothing is doing, in their estimation, unless brisk sparking is going on; and it is the long winters, with their sociable evenings, that do the mischief. Then it is that Lucy gets a beau home rather regularly, and her not-so-fortunate sisters of course laugh at her. Afterwards, if her "feller" feels inclined to turn it into serious business, he opens with a course of carefully timed visits, varying both in length and frequency, from once every two weeks to twice every one week. Sunday offers the peculiarly favored evening, which, in the country, seems to be sacred to courtship. Many and many a Sunday night have I seen a single lone candle burning in this house and that, at an hour when none but honest travellers and legitimate lovers had any moral or natural right to be out on the road.

The "best room" of the farmer's house is open then, though both sunshine and fire-light be kept out through the rest of the week. Passing by leisurely and a little scrutinizingly, one might distinctly make out a head — perhaps a close pair of them — firmly set on a pair of good shoulders, across the paper window-shade, which a single glance tells him belongs to some well-known young farmer-fellow who lives not over two miles off. Besides, there is a tired horse that stands patient and solitary before the gate-posts, perhaps with a big checked blanket sprawled over his frame, and his head dropping down between his knees in drowsy meditation on this sort of service.

In time, courtship leads to marriage; it generally does. This event, in the family, is the cap-sheaf of all others. For its sake, the household willingly consents to be turned topsy-turvy. Or, if it is resolved to be as secret as possible with the affair, it is wonderful what a sight of pains is taken to bruit it about. These little secrets are the best known of all sorts of news. Any goose could guess in a minute that preparations for a wedding were going on.

And a Country Wedding — let me tell you, my dear friend — is something to wish to live to be present at. No make-believe about it; but a hearty affair, to which, when you go, you wish with untold regrets that you could have stayed a good while longer. It is not so much the event itself, as it is the ceremonial adjuncts in the way of fun and frolic, that makes the time pass so lightly; all the imaginary delights of Mahomet's paradise pale before the substantial pleasures of a wedding at the old homestead. There is a vast deal of kissing done at this particular time, as if some contagion had broken out just as soon as the minister had so solemnly tied the knot and taken his fee. And many a timid and bashful pair, naturally shy about exchanging expressions of mutual preference, suddenly spruce up their courage on coming to take parts in this scene, and somehow "pop the question" right there on the spot, without pausing to think what hurt them.

Then the newly married couple think about "settling down" for themselves; if they conclude not to "go out West" the first year, the husband either settles on the old home-place under his father, or else buys or hires a farm by himself, and at once enters on his work as readily as a duckling takes to water. This side of the picture of beginning life, as some of the farmers' girls begin it, is both poetic and refreshing. It has such a flavor of good sense, too. These are the girls who become the mothers of our MEN; — the men who build our steamships and lay our railways, — who are to raise the character of their own calling, — on whom our cities make regular drafts for the brain, and bone, and sinew by which they are sustained and strengthened, — and who carry close in their hearts and hands the hopes of the coming years.

—— Blessed are the men who can say their mothers were country girls. They at least are inheritors of health, — and, in these days, that is something. They have heard something in their youth, if they have not themselves seen it, about grass, and dew, and trees, and the sunrise and sunset; and these are objects that enter a great deal farther into the heart of human nature than worldly people, with poor souls, are apt to suppose.

FARMERS' SONS.

SINCE the farmers of the country give it substance and character to-day, we may expect their sons to make up the warp and woof of the community that is to flourish after we sleep in the dust.

In the city, boys are nothing like what boys used to be, say five-and-twenty years ago. They begin about where their fathers left off. But, back in the country, it is not exactly so. There the boys start nearly as their fathers — in many cases, as their grandfathers — started before them. They enjoy a few more privileges in a very general way, to be sure; but still they are forced to split the toughest sort of knots for their early living, and accustom themselves to hardships and privations which to city youth would be absolutely unendurable.

A farmer's son is a young fellow who carries his fortune in his hand. He inherits nothing, — if he be the one to leave the paternal roof,

— and feels, therefore, that he has everything to make, and nothing to lose. Disciplined by the hard knocks to which he has been forced to submit, and toughened by the constant exposure to all sorts of luck about him, with his purpose fixed steadily in his heart, he pushes along in life, and comes out *somehow* — no one can seem to tell how — just where nobody ever thought he would, and far ahead of the point which richer men's sons reach behind him.

The farmer's boy has a hard time of it from the beginning. As soon as he is big enough to be trusted out-doors alone, they send him on errands to the neighbors, set him running after the cows, make him carry the milk and the haymakers' luncheon, and practise all manner of ingenious expedients to keep him out of mischief between the house and the barn. He is an article of no particular, but of very general use. In the house and out of the house, he never fails to come in play.

If there is any churning to be done, straightway a long towel is rigged about his neck, and he dashes away at the old-fashioned churn as if he were in pursuit of his living in good earnest. If the cattle have got into the corn, he takes the old house-dog and sets out pell-mell after them, with a whoop and hurrah that echoes all about the yard. If the paths are to be shovelled through the newly fallen snow, he plunges in head-foremost, and wallows about till he is whiter than a venerable miller, from top to toe. When the spring winds from the south begin to blow over the hill-sides and uplands, and the farmer collects his forces to mark out his fields in long and billowy furrows, young Joe climbs to the back of gentle Old Dobbin, and both tug together patiently from morning till night to turn the moist earth with the shining ploughshare.

The work of the farmer's boy is never done, though it begins as soon as his father calls him in the morning. He washes his ruddy face under the pump-spout, in the summer mornings, or at the well in the yard, — combs his tangled hair with any sort of implement that can be turned to such account, and hurries off to the cow-yard to help about the milking. In the winter-time, this makes cold work enough for him, as he will testify by stamping on the barn-floor, or by knocking his boots together after the fashion of his elders. If it be summer, as soon as all the milk-pails have been filled, he starts off, whip in hand, to drive the milky mothers to the distant pasture, and you may hear the sharp crack of his lash, or the shrill echoes of his voice, for a long way down the silent country road. When he gets back to the house, his feet coated with sand, and the bottoms of his trousers bedraggled in the dew and grass, he has the stomach for just as much breakfast as they choose to set before him. Sometimes it is a basin of bread-and-milk; sweet, new milk, of course, and bread as brown as the tanned face and hands he exhibits at the table. Oftentimes, too, a bite of cold meat, or a piece of pie, to "top off with." Always it is what the young chap knows very well, by that time, how to eat, and eat with all the zest of which his young constitution is capable.

If he earns a few odd coppers, now and then, by running of errands for the neighbors, and can take such good care of them as that they will not burn in his pocket, you may put your hand on him as one destined to be a *rich man*, in good time, even if he comes to nothing more. Sometimes, however, he hoards these meagre earnings but for the annual "trainings" in May and September; on which occasions he makes lavish investments in card-gingerbread and spruce beer, washing down huge semi-circular bites of the former with gulps of the latter that would well-nigh choke the throat of an experienced town-pump. Or, perhaps, he lays up his money against the time when he shall want a new cap, a new suit, or a new pair of boots to begin the next winter in. He is taught *thrift* as naturally as talking. He observes that everybody about him is engaged in bartering, selling, trading, and scheming to "make things go," and he catches the spirit of the practice as quick as he would bring home the measles from the over-crowded school-room. Those of his own household teach him economy as soon as he can observe and reason. He early comes to find that his battle with the world will be single-handed, that the opposition will never relax, and that he will have to fight to the end to keep himself where men like generally to be thought standing.

All the smoky maxims that pertain to domestic economy and advancement, he has got by heart; and, mixed and jumbled up with them, is a mass of "Poor Richard's" worldly wisdom, which makes of the compound a body of axiomatic truth sufficient to stand him in hand for his entire lifetime. Stories which his great-grandfather used to tell with such a relish in *his* day, are stuffed in his memory, possibly to be set afloat again on a current of tradition that will delight his own children and great-grandchildren after him.

He learns the history of the old French War and the Revolution at his father's fireside; and it is the more vividly painted to his imagination with the aid of the glowing oak and hickory coals wherein he strives to locate the stirring battle-scenes. If his mother be the mother she should, and such as our best and greatest men have had from the beginning, he must know all about the Bible history in his very earliest days, and can probably tell you more even than you find you know yourself of Saul and David, and Samuel, and Joshua, and Absalom, and the prophet Daniel, and Queen Esther, and the carrying away into captivity. The old Dutch tiles about the fireplace are not, to be sure, to be found in the homestead whence he springs, but he holds as many pictures as were ever etched on them, ineradically impressed upon his youthful heart.

In summer, he rarely thinks of going to school after reaching his twelfth or fifteenth year, but buckles down to the busy season's work with as much energy as the best of them. First comes planting: that is, the fences having been previously repaired, and the stones carefully picked off the mowing-lands. Then it is hoeing; once, twice, thrice, when he makes his young back ache long before bed-time, trying to keep up with the older hands on the farm. Then, haying; and this is the year's carnival to him. No impatient chap in school looks forward more wistfully to the "letting out;" and he watches with wonderful closeness the clover and timothy as it ripens, and listens with such a gush of glad sympathy to the quail that whistles on the rail that rides the wall of the mowing-lot, and keeps asking and asking *when* the sharpened scythe is going to be put in. All the morning, at this time, he stands and turns the grindstone for the mowers; runs about the barns and out-buildings for some implement that has mysteriously gone astray; assists in harnessing the horses, and yoking and unyoking the cattle; carries the luncheons down into the hay-fields; rakes after the cart; turns the hay while it is curing; and frolics with dogs and boys, toward night, among the haycocks that dot the field, till his head swims almost too much to permit him to remember his own name.

In the very last days of July, and along through the month of August, he is busy beyond telling among the huckleberry bushes and blackberry vines. He secures quart upon quart of these luscious fruits, sometimes toiling in the company of nothing but his bread-and-cheese luncheon from the dewy sunrise till the fading sunset. He brings home stained fingers and full baskets, as the best proofs of his industry and perseverance. The berries not needed for family use he is permitted to sell; and the aggregate of these proceeds of his merchandising would be very likely to surprise you.

Baskets-full are lifted on to the stage-driver's box, every morning when he passes over the road; and the driver is as exact in making change for him as if he were an accredited agent of the Rothschilds or the Barings. Few are the delights which summer offers him so unalloyed for his young heart as these of his excursions in the pastures for berries. He always loves, in after life, to revert to these days of innocence, and lingers on them with the whole tenderness of his nature. When he comes to manhood and the carking cares of the world's business, how many times he wishes he could but go barefoot once more as he used to do among the bushes and along the river's bank, inspired with the most truly independent feeling of which his heart was then, or since has been capable.

A deal of *boyish love*, too, is made in these

halcyon days; under the apple-trees, and by the concealing stone walls, or in the dark shadows of a young walnut-tree, while Susy, or Lucy, or Jane is trying to pick the berries from the bushes he has broken for one of them. Many a tender little heart gives itself away forever in the midst of these sweet seclusions, shaping its whole future life by the heedless but innocent impulses of the hour.

Through these summer days, the farmer's boy is kept at work as long as there is any light for him to see by; and then, with a stomach full of bread-and-milk, he goes off tired and staggering to bed. A king might envy him his golden sleep, for then it is he is a king himself. If such sweet and dewy slumber would but fall on his lids when he becomes a man!

When the Harvest Time approaches, he feels that the end of his hard labor is drawing nigh. He counts up the turkeys to see what Thanksgiving is likely to offer in the shape of promises. He looks impatiently forward to the day when school will begin for the winter in the little school-house at the fork of the roads, and wonders who is to be the lucky man to teach and flog the boys of the district during the winter.

As he stalks through the fall stubble, he tears

his tender ankles and cuts his naked feet with its bristling edges, and goes too often bleeding to bed. Then, he has corn-stalks to cut and stack; potatoes to dig and lug to the cart; turnips to pull till his hands feel like a bed of nettles; and all the odd jobs and chores to attend to that concern house and barn together. Burs get worked into his hair, and cockles stick all over his clothes. His feet are bruised and sore, and he goes with a limp that compels pity at sight.

His winters are devoted to his schooling. He usually has four months of it; and this suffices him until he comes to manhood, when he can do as much or as little for himself as he chooses. He sits in a tight room, that is alternately as hot as an oven and as cold as an ice-house; cons his lessons in the humming style of the old times; repeats them with all the nasalities and pedantic mannerisms taught him by the "master;" has chilblains regularly, which he digs and pounds through his boots in the afternoons; and thus worries through a winter after methods he is taught to consider at least improving, if not intellectual.

Of a life like this, our city boys know nothing at all. When the young representatives of the two styles of existence chance to meet, it is chiefly to eye one the other with envy and contempt, and to keep their sympathies wide apart until they reach manhood. The country lad gapes and stares at the wonders of the town, and the city youth asks what kind of wood hickory is, and supposes every farmer's barn-yard keeps at least *one* cow on purpose to give cream.

Nearly all the foremost men in our large cities were once farmers' boys. They left home in quest of their fortunes; and it is just such excellent qualities as they bring with their characters, that enrich our cities with the real wealth that holds them fast and firm.

In his homespun suit, therefore, barefooted and gaping, the Farmer's Boy is not to be despised; no, nor overlooked even. What he lacks is Opportunity. When that comes to him, he makes a fit career for himself without a great deal of assistance. If he stays behind and cultivates the old farm, taking good care of the "old folks" in their age, he still acts his part well, and merits our true commendation. He is emphatically a son of the brightest promise, and his inheritance in our country is rich enough to make all other men envious.

THE HIRED MAN.

PERHAPS, on the whole, it is better that all our agriculturists are not born with a farm to their hands, as some other men are said to be, with a "silver spoon in their mouth." Many, if not most of them, are obliged to study all the economies and strain every energy to secure the coveted prize at all; but, putting this single prize before them, they think, care, and live for nothing else, save to reach the limit of their aims just as quickly as they can. Early and late, in sickness and in health, in season and out of season, by self-denials and sacrifices uncounted, by patience and a perseverance that never faints through loneliness and personal privation, they labor hard to the end, like gold-hunters for the buried gift that is to flood their world with sunshine. No man can tell them, either, how many cents make a dollar, nor how many dollars it is going to take to buy the farm on which they have set their hopes and hearts.

Since the great West has opened wide its gates, the laboring men who fight these hand-to-hand battles with Fortune, have nearly all become emigrants, seeking the easier road to competence that lay open to them there; yet plenty are left behind to maintain the character of the old class, and to illustrate the names of such as I am about to describe.

When a working-man lets himself out to a Northern farmer, he contracts generally for the season of farm-work, — which includes planting, hoeing, haying, and harvesting, — or else makes his bargain for the year. In the first instance, he gets from twelve to sixteen dollars per month, with his board, — or, if he enjoys a local reputation for being "uncommonly likely help," he can command even more; since a good man's services are worth more in haying-time than in any other season. But if he lets himself by the year, as a good share of farmers' help do, he rarely rises beyond twelve dollars a month, with board added. During much of the winter season, a working-man's help is of little value. The most he can do is to milk, go to mill, chop and haul wood, and do the chores about the house. The women call on him to go out and fetch in a forestick, or roll in a backlog. Sometimes he sits down on a stool and churns for them. Sometimes it is one thing, and sometimes another. He may be always busy, but his work is nowise hard, and makes little or no show of immediate advantage to his employer.

Much of the farmers' help, at the present time, is made up of Irish laborers, — the unadulterated, unqualified bog-trotters of their native land. Yet they have not altogether crowded Yankee laborers out of the field; they have hardly more than stepped into the vacancies created by the Western fever that has carried so many off. Our farmers can do no better than to hire them. Now and then, one turns up a prize, but the bulk of them would as soon plant their potatoes in pits, on the day they handle their wages and leave, as on the day they first landed. In harnessing a horse, they would as soon throw the breeching over his head as over that part of his body which is ornamented with the tail.

—— The life of the *native* hired-man, drudging and wearisome as it looks to the careless observer, is still full of hope and buoyancy. He is not the friendless, melancholy, pitiful creature you may take him for. While he sits there in the chimney-corner of the old kitchen, telling stories to the boys in a low tone, so as not to be overheard, the honest blaze of the fire shining out over his bronzed face, he is as much a king and lord as the man of the acres who hires him. He keeps no cares on his mind, but can take his candle and go off to bed in his stocking-feet with the certainty of sleeping as soundly as the house-dog before the fire. Possibly he thinks of Home; but it only makes him all the more determined and resolute to work out, *somehow*, a home of his own.

In his mind, the future is mapped out as distinctly as any man's. He counts over his savings almost every day, knows just how much he put aside last month, how much he will this month, and what amount still stands between the present day and that on which he will realize his desires. He is ever hopeful; and, being hopeful, of course cheerful. The children love to hang around him, and you can hardly drive them away. Chestnuts, walnuts, slippery-elm bark, or something else, he has for all of them. He can tell them stories, or sing and whistle for them. Ghost-stories are his especial hobby, as they are likewise the delight of the younger ones, who swarm at his chair like bees at the doors of their hive. In their eyes, he is the wonder of a hero, and they really believe his past experience is such as was never paralleled.

He sleeps in a chamber off by himself, generally over the kitchen, — small and scantily furnished, with not a sign of a carpet on the floor, and perhaps only a bit of a broken mirror tacked against the wall. The rats and mice run at random about his head through the long nights of winter, kicking up racket enough to rain down the ceiling, but not disturbing him. He has earned his sleep, and not even a brigade of rats, racing like cavalry horses, can cheat him out of its possession.

None are so weather-wise as he. He prognosticates with vastly more accuracy than the wooden vane on the barn-gable, and knows as much about storms of snow and rain as the clerk of the weather himself. It is his forte, in Virgil's phrase —

> " Ventos et varium cœli prædiscere morem."

The women go to him to know if it will do to wash to-morrow, and if it is likely to turn out good drying weather. He knows all the clouds "like a book;" and stands behind the house at sunset, and studies their signs like a scholar before an algebraic problem on the blackboard. At such times, he seems to bear a close relation to the mysteries of Nature, as if he might have been chosen — without others knowing it — their high-priest and interpreter

The children think so, at any rate. They believe that if ever *any* man knew it all, it is he. And why ought it not to be as they believe? He studies with the confidence of simplicity, and trusts with all the faith of a child.

Perhaps there is a ruddy maid-servant living under the same roof. Perhaps, again, he has a "hankerin' notion" after that ruddy maid-servant. If so, the history of a single winter's sparking campaign at the kitchen fireplace is worthy to employ the pen that sketched the immortal siege of the Widow Wadman,— she with the troublesome eye. How he sits and pares apples over the same bowl with her, his hand touching her hand now and then, and her cheeks vieing with the very glow that lies abed beneath the forestick! How coyly she busies herself over the stocking she is knitting, casting occasional sheep's-eyes over at him, and persuading her thumping heart that he is a fine, stout, strapping farmer fellow, after all, and would make her one of the best of husbands — if she can but secure him!

How sharp she watches him while he whittles, wondering what it can be he is making for the boys, and secretly wishing he would take it in his head to carve out some trifling keepsake for *her!*

But before winter is done, he and she have managed to establish a good many confidences. He has let out some of his ulterior plans in life to her, and she has seen fit to be equally candid with him. These little recitals have had the effect, of course, to draw both closer together, and to make a sort of joint-stock of their general sentiments. While he has been holding skeins of yarn for her to wind, there is no telling how many times their eyes have exchanged expressive glances, nor what he may have dropped to her in a low voice, as often as the thread got entangled. When they both sat and stared at the glowing bed of coals at night, it is easy enough to conjecture that they saw a house and lands all pictured out in the fiery mass, and to infer that, concerning that house, they had indulged in many interesting speculations. If each chanced to like the other, the road to a match was smooth and easy; but if the partiality was developed as yet but on one side, it was indescribably amusing to watch the turns, the shifts, the innocent prevarications, and the daily manœuvring, that were employed to stimulate the esteem of the dilatory party. Sly hints — unseen kindnesses — long breaths and sighs — sidelong glances — and melancholy looks were put under tribute with all possible industry, and kept in constant and vigorous use until the field was finally won.

The hired man reads the agricultural papers now; once, he would never have thought of such a thing. Instead of being kept down to firelight, he has the use of a candle; and there is many and many a hard-working fellow who had not a dollar with which to face the round world at the start, saving what he made through the day, and treasuring up what he read at night, who now owns his farm clear of mortgages of any grade, and wields an honest influence second to that of no man in his locality. He did it simply by persevering: that is the way the soft water-drops wear holes in the hard rock, at last. He did it by shutting out every other thought and purpose from his view, and pursuing only that object which he had thus set before himself in his early youth. He made up his mind, with God's blessing, to reach his mark, and he reached it. Any one can conquer, in the battle of life, if he buckles on his armor in a similar spirit.

If he earns a hundred and fifty dollars each year, with his board added, he means to save a hundred and twenty-five of it, if he can. Plenty of them do it, too. In this patient way, working year in and year out with unflagging perseverance, he presently manages to make a beginning towards his farm, and is willing to buy with a mortgage on his shoulders, trusting to good health and hard work to redeem his indebtedness and enable him to stand clear of all incumbrances finally. Whether he pays down five, seven, or ten hundred dollars to begin with, he means to clear up his bushes and mortgages as fast as he can, and be at length his own master.

Or, he sometimes only *hires* a farm, and stocks it with the means he has managed to scrape together. In such case, he takes to wife the girl whom he has all along been courting at the kitchen fire, and they at once move in and set up housekeeping. The elder farmers, of assured estates, show him a good deal of patronage at meeting and in the store, addressing him by his Christian name and asking him how he is getting along. But his upper lip takes on more decided expression as year is added to year, and he lives along with nursing his silent resolution to be even with them by and by. It is nothing — the whole of it — but a struggle for money, just as the boys strive for marbles and jack-straws; and it is off the same piece, out in the sweet country, that one studies the pattern of so closely, in hustling Wall Street.

Few, however, get to be forehanded very soon, in hiring a farm in this way; all who do must needs be most industrious workers. They must keep at it from cock-crow till early moonrise, the year round. They have to work hard, eat hard, and sleep hard; it is the hard dollars they are after. Even all this will not secure the prize, health being thrown in beside, unless intelligence presides at the board, and gives shape to their industry. They must keep fully abreast with the times, at any rate; and these are the most wide-awake times the world was ever confused with yet. They must know a little something about the results of experiments in agricultural chemistry. They must be ready to adopt the real improvements in agricultural machinery. They cannot be unmindful of the best theories relative to the rotation of crops, and the soundest ideas relative to manures. They must be ready to assail the buried wealth of their swamp lands, and drag up the hidden gold to the surface. Artificial irrigation, too, will pay for attending to, that promising fields may not yearly be left to burn up and perish. They must sit down and estimate the practical value, *to them,* of root culture in furnishing feed for stock, in its combination with the old-style rules of providing animal subsistence in plenty. They are to understand, at the start, the nature of their soils, — what they lack, and how and in what quantities the lack is best supplied. Nor may they quite shut their eyes to the plain road to competency by the raising of orchard fruits — apples, pears, and quinces; this is a mine of wealth which our farmers have been too slow to go and open. They must think it either pottering or dangerous. When they once wake up to it as an important item in their own business, our unsupplied millions will have fruit enough to become both juicier and healthier than now.

The hired man's life, with our Northern farmers, is but an apprenticeship. Some of them emerge from it to pass to the dignity of proprietorship; while a great many more continue in harness, tugging at the traces, and dragging out a solitary existence to the end of their days. They lie about, here and there, jobbing as the opportunity offers; laboring one season in this place, and another season in that; now laying by a trifle, and now saving scarce a penny; good-natured and trustful generally; as dry and smoky as the soot that collects about their favorite chimney-corners; troubling themselves nowise with care or ambition; as full of gossip as old ladies over their fragrant Oolong decoctions, and addicted to a garrulousness that, to all the children where they go, is as delightful as a new story-book. Bachelors they live, and bachelors they die; and, as a matter of course, living but half their natural days.

Odd sticks in the bundle they are, incapable of being either tied up or assorted. Needful to the farmer, yet profitless, so far as results reach, to themselves. A happy, hard-working, necessary, favorite class of men.

THE TURKEY NEST

Out in the lots, just under the edge
Of some birches that hide a ragged ledge,
An old hen turkey has made a nest
Of dried oak-leaves about her breast,
And there she sits by herself all day, —
Sits and sits from April to May.
She has stolen off from the flock at home,
And out to this lonely spot has come
To raise, unseen, her summer brood
Of speckled poults in the sweet green wood.
The boys have all in vain essayed
To find where the sly and secret old jade
Her nest of eggs has securely laid;
And the gobbler saunters off all alone,
To see where the lady has really gone: —
But there she sits on her spotted eggs,
Heaped up so warm beneath her legs, —
Sits under her thatch of pale green leaves,
That shed the drops like a farmer's eaves,
Through damps and mists and cloudy weather,
Without ever so much as wetting a feather,
In the midst of the music of April rains,
And the bursting of flowers all over the plains,

And the sweet green grass, that steadily creeps
Across the meadows and up to the steeps, —
Sits and watches, and sits and sleeps.

Her liquid eye, so full and so bright,
Is like some jewel that 's swimming with light;
And everywhere in its great round rim
Is packed with motherly love to the brim.
She spies the hawk in his highest flight,
And the thieving skunk in the darkest night;
And when the owl whoops out its cry,
She winks and blinks and looks up at the sky,
Crooning her fierce anxiety.
What is she thinking of, lone squatter there,
Thinking and winking, through foul and through
fair?
Squirrels chattering up in the trees,
Pirates of crows bearing down in the breeze,
Portly old wookchucks passing her door —
Now on their hind-feet, and now on all four;
Rabbits listening to hear where 's the noise
That comes from the dogs in the wood with the
boys;
Robins in haste, with their mouths full of mud,
Dug from the marge of some little spring flood;
Brown thrushes pouring melodious notes,
Not all their own, but from out their own throats;
A fox, now and then, flitting by like a ghost,
And a chipmonk laughing to see the scamp post;
Bumble-bees leaving a long trail of song,

And gay-coated insects, a murmuring throng;
Runlets trickling from ledge to ledge
To water the roots of sprouting sedge;
All patterns of clouds on the blue of the sky,
Woven by shuttles that wind-fingers ply, —
All through the Spring nights, out under the stars,
Orion or Pleiades, Venus or Mars,
She thinks, and she winks, with her motherly breast
Down on the heap of her warm treasures pressed.

She thinks of the chicks that will start and run, —
Eighteen, twenty, or twenty-one, —
Of how they will troop with her off in the dews,
Yawping till even her heart they confuse,
Up the green hill-sides, through forests of ferns,
And down where the little brook tangles and turns,
Roaming at will through the long summer day,
From the moment the dawn bids them up and away,
And sleeping at night where the night overtakes them,
Huddled and safe in the bed that she makes them,
Till, waxing in strength, they scale the stone walls,
And on all the farmers make regular calls, —
Now hid in their corn-fields, now trampling their oats,

Skulking, and yelping, and cramming their throats, —
In the woods, after acorns just out of the cup,
Off in the lots, snapping grasshoppers up,
Getting thick on the thighs and stout on the
breast,
And seeming to see which will turn out the best.

And the old turkey thinks that the time then will
come,
When through the still woods sounds the partridge's drum,
The chill autumn nights will give hints to go
home;
When up in the apple-trees near the back-door,
With sky for a roof and bare boughs for a floor,
Or perched on the ridge of the barn or the shed,
All squat in a row, head close up to head,
They doze through the nights till the first streak
of dawn
Calls them down from their roosts for their ration
of corn.
And, soon after, comes the good Thanksgiving
Day,
When the winter of age takes the green on of
May,
And all spirits are back in the homestead at play:
Upon the long table that 's spread in the room,
Padded out with many a savory crumb,
Heads off their shoulders and wings skewered
down,

Legs in the air and breasts roasted brown, —
There lie two of these poults, each on a broad
platter,
While over them rings the loud family clatter.

And but to the end of this glad sacrifice
To the annual call of the Home Deities,
Do the chicks ever pick through the walls of
their shell,
Or grow fat in the woods, on the steelyards to
tell
What a weight of sweet meat they are able to
score,
And bring it upon their own backs to the door,
As turkeys have done, generations before:
The Thanksgiving feast would be no great affair,
Except this dear carcass were prominent there;
Of the "fat and the sweet" that help give the day
zest,
The choicest part comes from the old Turkey
Nest.

THE END.

www.ingramcontent.com/pod-product-compliance
Lightning Source LLC
LaVergne TN
LVHW010202110826
845151LV00002B/583

* 9 7 8 1 4 2 5 5 3 6 1 5 2 *